Teaching and Learning in the Digital Age

Teaching and Learning in the Digital Age is for all those interested in considering the impact of emerging digital technologies on teaching and learning. It explores the concept of a digital age and perspectives of knowledge, pedagogy and practice within a digital context.

By examining teaching with digital technologies through new learning theories cognisant of the digital age, it aims to both advance thinking and offer strategies for teaching technology-savvy students that will enable meaningful learning experiences.

Illustrated throughout with case studies from across the subjects and the age range, key issues considered include:

- How young people create and share knowledge both in and beyond the classroom and how current and new pedagogies can support this level of achievement.
- The use of complexity theory as a framework to explore teaching in the digital age.
- The way learning occurs – one way exchanges, online and face-to-face interactions, learning within a framework of constructivism, and in communities.
- What we mean by critical thinking, why it is important in a digital age, and how this can occur in the context of learning.
- How students can create knowledge through a variety of teaching and learning activities, and how the knowledge being created can be shared, critiqued and evaluated.

With an emphasis throughout on what it means for practice, this book aims to improve understanding of how learning theories currently work and can evolve in the future to promote truly effective learning in the digital age. It is essential reading for all teachers, student teachers, school leaders, those engaged in Masters' level work, as well as students on Education Studies courses.

Louise Starkey is Associate Dean in Primary and Secondary Education at Victoria University of Wellington, New Zealand.

Teaching and Learning in the Digital Age

Louise Starkey

Routledge
Taylor & Francis Group

LONDON AND NEW YORK

First published 2012
by Routledge
2 Park Square, Milton Park, Abingdon, Oxon OX14 4RN

Simultaneously published in the USA and Canada
by Routledge
711 Third Avenue, New York, NY 10017

Routledge is an imprint of the Taylor & Francis Group, an informa business

British Library Cataloguing in Publication Data
A catalogue record for this book is available from the British Library

Library of Congress Cataloging-in-Publication Data
Starkey, Louise.
Teaching and learning in the digital age / Louise Starkey.
    p. cm.
Includes bibliographical references and index.
1. Educational technology. 2. Education—Effect of technological innovations on.
3. Digital communications. I. Title.
LB1028.3.S737 2012
371.33–dc23   2011048336

ISBN: 978-0-415-66362-5 (hbk)
ISBN: 978-0-415-66363-2 (pbk)
ISBN: 978-0-203-11742-2 (ebk)

Typeset in Galliard
by Cenveo Publisher Services

Printed and bound in Great Britain by
TJ International Ltd, Padstow, Cornwall

Contents

List of figures and tables   viii
Introduction   x
Acknowledgements   xiii

1 The complexity of schools   1
   Complexity theory 1
   The context of a complex organisation 3
   Emerging knowledge through connections 4
   Diversity and redundancy 5
   Balancing randomness and deterministic order 6
   Complexity theory and change in schools 8
   Summary 9

2 The digital age   10
   The industrial age 10
   The digital age 14
   Global significance 16
   Summary 19

3 Knowledge and connectivism   20
   Perspectives of knowledge 20
   Knowledge and learning theories 22
   Connectivist learning theory 26
   Curriculum 26
   Summary 28

4 Connections and relationships   29
   Teacher–student connection 29
   Connections with peers 32
   Connections within the learning context 34
   Connections beyond the classroom 36
   Connections within learning 38
   Summary 39

5   **Creating knowledge**   41
    Concepts 41
    Knowledge building 42
    Knowledge products 43
    Conceptual artefacts 45
    Knowledge creation 47
    Summary 54

6   **Critical thinking**   55
    Critical thinking 55
    Critical thinking about information, data and resources 57
    Critical thinking while learning concepts and skills 58
    Critical thinking about learning progress 59
    Critical thinking and creating knowledge 63
    Critical thinking and assessment 63
    Summary 66

7   **Learning in the digital age**   68
    Motivation 68
    Examples of digital age learning experiences 71
    Telling a story 71
    Poetry 73
    Language learning 76
    Atoms and molecules 78
    Elite performance 81
    Why does my city looks like it does? 84
    Artistic messages 86
    Back to the future 87
    Summary 90

8   **Teaching in the digital age**   92
    Prioritising teaching or learning 92
    Pedagogical reasoning 93
    Content knowledge 94
    Pedagogical content knowledge 95
    Knowledge of educational psychology 96
    Knowledge of learners 97
    Contextual knowledge 98
    Evidence of learning progress 99
    Teaching for mastery learning 99
    Diversity in learning 101
    Evidence based teaching 102
    Analysis 103
    Using evidence with students 104

Teaching in the virtual learning environment 105
Summary 106

9   **The start of the digital age**   **107**
Digital age curriculum 107
Implications for teachers 110
Implications for students 114
Implications for schools 117
Implications for the national or state policy makers 120
Complexity theory and the process of change 124
Summary 126

Notes   128
References   129
Index   135

Figures and tables

Figures

1.1	Complexity theory applied to a school context	2
1.2	Simplified levels within a complex organisation	3
1.3	Connections from a teacher's perspective within a complex organisation	4
1.4	Complexity within schools as a new technology is introduced	6
1.5	Balancing randomness and deterministic order	7
1.6	Innovations or new ideas influence systemic processes, structures or knowledge	7
1.7	Stable systemic knowledge	8
2.1	Education and complexity in the industrial age	13
2.2	Complexity and evolving curricular	14
3.1	The relationship between epistemology and schooling	21
3.2	Positivist perspective	23
3.3	Constructivist perspective	23
3.4	Connectivist perspective	25
3.5	Comparison of knowledge and teaching in the digital and industrial ages	27
4.1	Teacher–student learning relationship	31
4.2	Student problem solving during learning – making connections	33
4.3	Example of a behaviour management plan focused on student learning	36
4.4	Place based learning – connecting with the local community	37
5.1	Examples of concepts	42
5.2	Taxonomies to build conceptual knowledge or skills	43
5.3	Assessment rubric focused on task goals	44
5.4	Assessment rubric focused on learning goals	45
5.5	Learning, mastery and knowledge creation	50
5.6	Learning in the digital age	51
5.7	Home economics learning in the digital age	52
6.1	Badverts' evaluation rubric	61
6.2	Plan for self regulated learning	62
6.3	Teacher critique	64
6.4	Peer critique	65
6.5	Critique for knowledge creation	66
7.1	Expectancy-value theory	69

7.2   Expectancy-value theory of a wannabe skier   69
7.3   Expectancy-value theory of wannabe skier after first day   69
7.4   Framework for learning   70
7.5   Framework for learning storytelling   72
7.6   Storytelling learning experience model   73
7.7   Framework for poetry learning experience   75
7.8   Poetry learning experience model   76
7.9   Conversation learning experience model   78
7.10 Conversation learning experience model   79
7.11 Framework for learning experience, atoms and molecules   80
7.12 Atoms and molecules learning experience model   81
7.13 Sports coaching framework for learning   83
7.14 Sports coaching learning experience model   83
7.15 Urban spatial patterns framework for learning   85
7.16 Urban spatial patterns learning experience model   86
7.17 Artistic message learning framework   87
7.18 Artistic messages learning experience model   88
7.19 Back to the future learning framework   90
7.20 Back to the future learning experience model   90
8.1   The teacher scream   93
8.2   Pedagogical reasoning and action in the digital age   94
8.3   Value-expectancy theory   96
8.4   Evidence based teaching practice   99
8.5   Learning experiences   100
8.6   Differentiated learning outcomes in teacher centred model of schooling 102
8.7   Differentiated learning outcomes in learner centred model of schooling 102
9.1   Progression of learning of a concept or skill as a basis for assessment 109
9.2   Student timetable   116
9.3   Schools developing and sharing knowledge within society   118
9.4   Pendulum of state accountability of schooling outcomes   121
9.5   Pendulum balance to evidence based professional accountability   121
9.6   Assessment in the digital age   123
9.7   Complexity of schooling   125
9.8   Conditions of emergent knowledge   126

Table

2.1   Enrolment at high school, selected countries in 1867 (Connell, 1980)   11

Introduction

In the past few decades a number of books and articles have been published about teaching with digital technologies, with useful insights into how teachers and schools can integrate or introduce computer programmes, information and communications technology (ICT), learner management systems, or student management systems into the classroom or schooling sector. Another body of literature ponders the future of schools with the opportunities that network and online learning offer, or how theories underpinning learning and schooling systems might evolve as people are connected through flexible communication networks. Other authors have considered how the emerging generation of children might be different to previous generations and social fiction writers have considered what society might be like in a digital age. This book combines some of these ideas to consider how teaching and learning might be in a digital age.

As an author, I bring a perspective that is based on my experiences as a student, teacher, school leader and educational researcher within New Zealand. The perspective I bring is constantly evolving as I read, discuss and interact within social and professional contexts. Living in a country with a relatively small population base means that there is a focus on global trends, ideas and research, which are viewed through a New Zealand lens.

This book is written at the start of the digital age and reflects emerging and established ideas of this time. An example of the time of writing is the metaphors and choice of adjectives to explain ideas of knowledge and learning are drawn from the biological sciences (e.g. complexity, evolving), and manufacturing or industry (e.g. construct, network). As society evolves in the digital age different metaphors and perspectives will evolve perhaps from physics or sociology and this will give further insight into how teaching and learning may occur.

Complexity theory provides a framework for considering how a system such as education changes and evolves over time which cannot be reduced to simple cause and effect due to the multiple levels of influences. This has made the explanation of complexity theory problematic. I have used models and metaphors to explain how the theory might be applied to compulsory education in the digital age, and in doing so I have focused on aspects of the theory but inevitably have not been able to always capture the complexity.

The scene is set for this book in the first chapter by examining schools as complex organisations through which knowledge emerges. This chapter outlines complexity theory as applied to schools, including the following constructs:

- Complex systems are multileveled, ambiguously bound and cannot be examined as isolated parts.

- The connections between the parts are where knowledge emerges.
- Change is not predictable, but the balance between randomness and deterministic order influenced by historical experiences.

Complexity theory is used as a framework to examine how the introduction of digital technologies to society is resulting in a change in teaching in subsequent chapters.

The second chapter examines the digital age. It situates the digital age in an historical context by comparing the influence that the Industrial Revolution had on schooling. What is meant by the digital age is examined and the impact that this is having on society. This leads on to the influence digital technologies are having on teenage cultural practices and their use in schools at the start of the digital age.

The third chapter provides a discussion of the changing notion of knowledge, beliefs and learning theories. It leads to an outline of connectivist learning theory as a theory relevant to the digital age.

The fourth chapter links the digital age with complexity theory through an exploration of the importance of connections between parts of the system including information, data systems and people. The process of learning or developing knowledge involves connecting information, datum, concepts or ideas. This occurs within the mind of the individual, between people as a group seeks to gain a shared understanding and can lead to knowledge creation where unique outcomes are developed and shared. Relationships within the class-room and beyond establish the connections through which learning is explored, developed and discussed. This chapter explores the importance of learning relationships within a schooling setting.

The fifth chapter explores a key development within teaching and learning theory for the digital age, which is the way that students can be creating and sharing knowledge beyond classroom walls. The approach taken is to examine creativity, and then explore how students can create knowledge through a variety of teaching and learning activities and how the knowledge being created can be shared, critiqued and evaluated.

Critically examining sources of information, information, emerging knowledge and the process of learning are core for the digital age learner and therefore the teacher. The sixth chapter is an exploration of what critical thinking is, why it is important in a digital age, and how this can occur in the context of teaching.

Student learning motivation is an important aspect of teaching and learning. A range of learning experiences underpinned by digital age learning theory and designed with student motivation in mind are outlined in the seventh chapter with the purpose of explor-ing how students might experience school learning in the digital age. These include examples from science, physical education, English, literacy, geography, language learning, art and integrated curriculum. Across the examples a range of pedagogical approaches are included.

The teaching process is explored in the eighth chapter. Effective teachers in the digital age context will be part of a highly skilled profession focused on student learning. The teachers will have strong content knowledge appropriate for the level and subjects being taught, pedagogical content knowledge, the ability to cement learning relationships, and understand how to gather, analyse and apply learning data within their teaching practice. Digital innovations provide communication tools, electronic evidence management and analyses systems and will continue to be developed to enable and enhance the process of teaching and learning.

The final chapter explores the implications of digital age teaching and learning on aspects of the education system. There are implications for curricular, teachers and what it means to be a teacher, students, schooling structures and schooling policies. In complex systems such as education these are posited as ideas or scenarios. This concluding chapter situates the ideas of the book within the start of the digital age, a time when teachers, teacher educators and researchers are beginning to explore how teaching and learning in the digital age may develop.

Acknowledgements

This book has only been possible through the support, mentoring and guidance from colleagues, family and friends and the learning experiences of being a student, learning from students as a teacher and teacher educator. I would like to acknowledge the valuable feedback I received from Azra Moeed, Barrie Gordon, Mark Sheehan, Shelley Gilman, Tara Evans and Gillian Hubbard during the writing process. I would also like to acknowledge the generous support received from Victoria University of Wellington with the time, resources and encouragement to complete the writing of this book, including access to the expertise of Jane Barrett, Anna Thompson, Irene Sattar and Cheryl Moon who developed the diagrams.

Chapter 1

The complexity of schools

Schools are complex places and learning is a complex process. This chapter outlines the perspective through which educational or schooling systems are considered within this book. Complexity theory underpinned the way that research is considered, experiences are framed, and the thinking about how teaching and learning might occur within the digital age.

Educational systems are organised with multilevel structures (classes, year levels, departments, timetables, and calendars), they include a range of participants (students, teachers, governors or administrators, leaders, policy makers, families, communities, and agencies), and are required to meet an assortment of changing expectations (social, professional, achievement, and financial). Complexity theory offers a framework to consider teaching and learning in the digital age within the context of schooling and educational systems.

Complexity theory

In 2000 Stephen Hawking predicted that the next century would be the century of complexity (Chui, 2000). Over time theories are reviewed and new ideas and ways of examining society emerge based on concepts relevant to the time and context. Complexity theory has emerged from the physical sciences where exploration of how communities of organisms change is focused on the complexity of the systems rather than individual cause and effect processes within a deterministic universe. The theory is being applied to the social sciences to examine how complex systems, such as education, evolve and develop over time.

Complexity theory has a number of interrelated constructs which can be explored through examining context, structures, catalysts for change, and knowledge creation processes within an organisation or system (Figure 1.1).

A complex system or organisation consists of a number of levels, with each level having a recognisable open boundary (Waldrop, 1992). At each level there are connections between the parts where knowledge emerges through interaction. There are many organisational levels in a school setting. Schools have formal structures, which may include classes, year levels, subject based departments, syndicates, teacher committees, leadership groups and governance boards. Figure 1.2 illustrates a few of the levels that can exist within a schooling system. Each of these levels has its own set of knowledge and processes, which develop over time.

The boundaries of the levels within an organisation are open in that membership can change, information and ideas are exchanged beyond and between these levels, and the

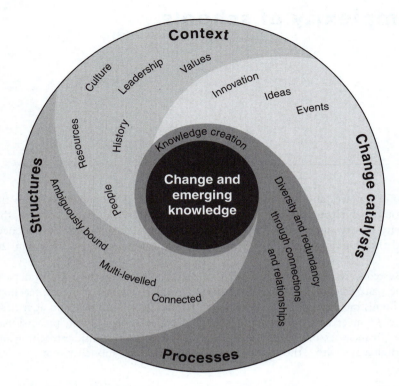

Figure 1.1 Complexity theory applied to a school context.

levels overlap with individuals and resources belonging to multiple levels. Experiences and knowledge gained from one level will be applied and shared at other levels. Therefore knowledge and ideas at one level are transferred to other levels. None of the levels are independent; they are connected so that events, ideas or innovations emerging through one level will potentially affect other levels.

A secondary school teacher is typically a member of one or more classes, they may belong to more than one subject department, be on the assessment committee and the curriculum committee, organise outdoor education and belong to the teaching staff (Figure 1.3). For example, an English teacher forms a connection with students and their families as they teach, lead extracurricular activities and discuss learning progress. The same teacher has connections with colleagues at school through formal and informal groups that they belong to, and as an English teacher they connect with other English teachers through subject based networks.

Schools belong to communities, districts and national schooling networks. Knowledge or ideas are exchanged beyond the organisational boundaries of a school, such as through regional or national subject teacher associations, principal networks and community events. Schools are ambiguously bound organisations. It is not possible (or desirable) to control how and what knowledge is exchanged within and across the boundaries, which contributes

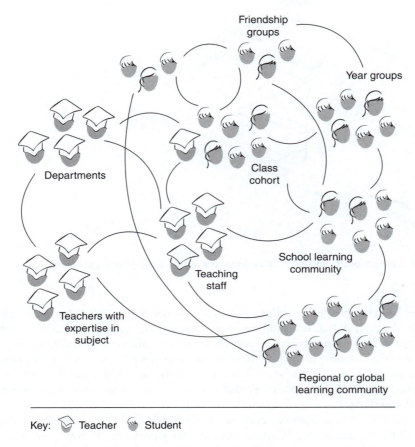

Key: Teacher   Student

Figure 1.2 Simplified levels within a complex organisation.

to the unpredictability of emerging knowledge and responses to changes within a complex system such as a school.

The context of a complex organisation

Each organisation or complex system operates in a unique context. The uniqueness is derived from the people, history and culture of the context. Each school has a range of employees, leaders, governors, students and families, each bringing differing beliefs, perspectives, expectations and experiences to their interactions within the school. Teachers have differing perspectives on pedagogical practices, which will filter how they perceive or implement a particular innovation within their teaching practice (this point is explored further in this book when considering teaching and learning with digital technologies). School leaders each have their own leadership style depending on their personality, knowledge, beliefs, experiences and the school context they are leading. The leadership influences

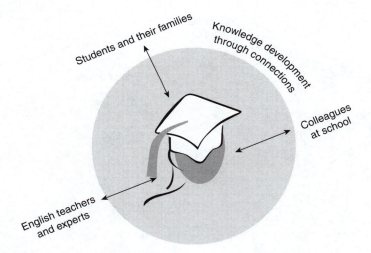

Figure 1.3 Connections from a teacher's perspective within a complex organisation.

how and what knowledge emerges within a school (Robinson *et al.*, 2009). A school leader can, through direct and indirect support of an innovation, encourage teaching staff, students and parents to engage with a change. A leader in a different school context may not verbally support the same innovation or introduce support processes, which can result in different value being put on the same innovation by the staff and students at the two different contexts. It is not only the leader that influences change but also the embedded organisational knowledge.

Complex systems or organisations draw on their history as they evolve over time (Buchanan, 2000). In a schooling context this includes knowledge of how a process of change has occurred in the past or particular values that have developed and underpin an organisation or the levels within an organisation. Each school has a unique culture that has emerged over its history through the people, events and the context in which it exists (Senge *et al.*, 2000) and each level within an organisation has a unique culture. For example, the way that the English department makes decisions about curriculum may differ from the science department. One may have a top-down approach that is focused on compliance; the other may have a consultative approach structured around negotiated department goals. The history of a school and the people within it influence the culture of a school, including the way that change occurs and how knowledge emerges.

Emerging knowledge through connections

Complexity theory is a way of considering how knowledge emerges within a complex organisation. Stacey (2001) noted that human relations lie at the heart of complexity theory where the agency and mutual influence of individuals and groups create a responsive process. Connections between individual, groups and resources across the organisational levels are where ideas, innovations and events are discussed, evaluated and sometimes modified and embedded. It is through these connections that knowledge emerges, building or modifying what is known by the collective group. Knowledge can emerge through conversations between teachers in a school or department, discussions with parents, reading of research, examining data, meetings, online information exchange with other educationalists or conversations in the classroom setting. Participants in the system respond to the context, thereby changing the context while developing their own ideas and knowledge (Davis and Sumara, 2006). While schools, education systems and classrooms can appear to be top-down driven, there is research that reflects how the relationships, history and culture within each level influences change from the bottom up (Bishop and Glynn, 1999; Senge *et al.*, 2000; Wink, 2000). Emerging knowledge is influenced by the parts, participants and processes within the system.

Morrison (2002) examined complexity theory within the context of schools and school leadership. He noted that by limiting research within schools to the individual parts, the whole picture can be misunderstood. He proposed that it is impossible to predict what the outcomes of one aspect of change will be in a school as there are so many connections that will influence the response.

Connections occur at multiple levels including external connections between people or devices and internal connections made during the learning process. John Dewey noted that when learning, perceptions cannot be separated from judgements as isolated aspects of learning do not make sense until they are connected within a wider context. Connections are an important aspect of learning and knowledge creation.

Diversity and redundancy

A complex system like a school is in a state of constant change with the regular introduction or emergence of new ideas, innovations and events. If every suggestion, idea or proposal was implemented the school would be in a state of chaos. Therefore complex organisations go through processes of evaluating, disregarding and trialling innovations and new ideas, which creates diversity of practice, ideas and systems. Other innovations and longstanding practices or ideas become redundant and are discontinued or replaced. Consider an example of an innovation such as the introduction of a digital technology (for example netbooks) for students (Figure 1.4). Such an introduction could create change in practices in the school, and from this knowledge will emerge. It would not be predictable exactly what will change as it will depend on contextual factors such as the beliefs and knowledge of individuals and groups, current practices, resources and interactions across the organisation. New understandings (or knowledge) will emerge through the connections between the parts of the organisation as experiences and ideas are discussed and shared. With the introduction of a netbook other practices or ideas may become redundant, such as the use of paper student diaries, the need for student lockers, the idea that all students in a class must be physically present in the classroom to be participating interactively in the learning. Diversity and redundancy are likely to be unique to each specific context dependent on the history, culture and other variables such as the preferences and experiences of teachers, values and beliefs and the resourcing available. Through this process of diversity and redundancy, knowledge emerges through connections in complex organisations.

Complexity exists between deterministic order and randomness, the place referred to as the 'edge of chaos'. It is logical that when a system is closer to the edge of chaos there is likely to be increased levels of redundancy and diversity within the processes and practices than found in a stable controlled environment. Conditions of emergent learning within a

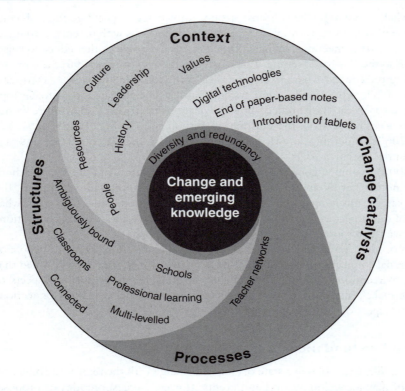

Figure 1.4 Complexity within schools as a new technology is introduced.

classroom setting were examined through the application of a complexity theory (Sullivan, 2009). Emergent learning was found to occur in a classroom environment on the edge of chaos, where students had a sense of agency and the learning context was loosely bound. This compared to a classroom with a tightly bound learning environment where the edge of chaos was avoided and there was minimal student agency. In this latter context emergent learning was undetectable.

Balancing randomness and deterministic order

A complex system is not static, which adds to its unpredictability when faced with a change. A complex organisation faces ongoing change in its structures, participants, parts, processes and knowledge. In a schooling environment there are pupils (and their families) joining and leaving, staff changes, changing curriculum, resources updated, new content knowledge to teach, district or national policy changes, emerging knowledge from research and practitioner experience and many other changes, all of which contribute to the complexity of the context. The resulting changes are a balance between randomness and deterministic order (Cilliers, 1998).

Schools are influenced by apparent randomness such as technological innovations, natural events, government policy initiatives and societal changes, which create pressure for

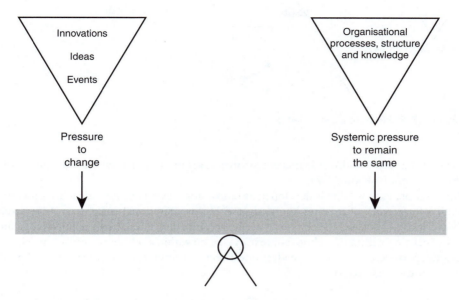

Figure 1.5 Balancing randomness and deterministic order.

change within the system. They are also influenced by deterministic pressures such as systems knowledge, routines and values. The pressure to change or innovate acts like a counterweight to the pressure to remain the same (Figure 1.5). It is through the apparent randomness and deterministic order that knowledge emerges, as ideas or innovations become part of organisational knowledge.

When the pressures of new ideas, events or innovations outweigh deterministic order new knowledge can emerge within a system. In a system such as a school that is close to the edge of chaos the deterministic order is less influential and the decision makers may be more receptive to initiatives or new ideas. For example, a school with a diverse population that gives a voice to all the groups within the school might operate on the edge of chaos with the pressure to implement innovations stronger than the systemic pressure to remain the same (Figure 1.6).

This is unlikely to occur if the context is in a state of chaos, or will occur to a lesser extent if it is far from the edge of chaos. The pressure for deterministic order is likely to be strong

Figure 1.6 Innovations or new ideas influence systemic processes, structures or knowledge.

Figure 1.7 Stable systemic knowledge.

in a school that has top-down management structures predominating and the culture of a 'traditional school' (Figure 1.7).

Organisational knowledge is developed as innovations, events or new ideas are processed through a framework of existing knowledge within organisational structures. As apparent catalysts for change occur, the responses are underpinned or filtered by the knowledge and processes existing within the school context. A change within a school can cause participants to consider perspectives and explore ideas or different structures that further develop knowledge within the organisation.

Complexity theory and change in schools

In a study of computer use in two schools in Silicon Valley (USA) during 1998–99, it was concluded that the cost of investing in computers (in both time and money) had not been educationally worthwhile (Cuban *et al.*, 2001). They found very little use, with less than 5 per cent of teachers integrating computer technology into their teaching practice. Cuban *et al.* (2001) summarised that the teachers in his study adapted computer use to fit with their traditional practices rather than adapting the way they teach to take account of the opportunities offered by computers (as had been hoped by policy makers and some proponents of information communication technologies). The researchers had assumed that by studying schools in Silicon Valley they were likely to see computers being used to enhance learning. An assumption had been made that by placing computers into schools there would be significant change within the schools; a cause–effect relationship would be seen.

Complexity theory can be applied to the situation to examine schools as complex organisations. The context to which the computers were introduced had existing structures, values, processes and organisational knowledge. The different levels in the school would have considered what they do with this resource or innovation. The participants in the school communities will have drawn on a range of their existing knowledge and experiences including knowledge of pedagogical processes, learning theory and practices within the school and experiences of using, observing, discussing or reading about new technologies for teaching. Underpinning any decisions and discussions would be perspectives on the purpose of schooling, the job of teaching and the core values of the school. The way decisions were made would reflect the culture of the school and therefore be unique in each context. They would have been influenced by student conceptions of learning and the local and national expectations of teachers. Therefore the resulting change was tempered by the pressure for deterministic order, and the consequence of introducing computers in Silicon Valley schools, as with innovations in a complex system, was unpredictable.

Two other studies illustrate the complexity of change in schools. An in-depth study of teachers in Taiwan (Chen, 2008) found that most teachers surveyed identified with constructivist beliefs (which had been a government focus) but when observed teaching they tended to use digital technologies within a transmission practice rather than teach to encourage constructivist learning. A second study focused on a teacher who aimed to use digital technologies to help students learn in a constructivist way and found that while the teacher was designing collaborative knowledge construction activities the students were acculturated in a transmission style of learning, thereby creating a barrier to a new way of approaching their learning (Starkey and McCarthy, 2008). These examples show how the many different aspects within a complex organisation connect and interact to moderate innovations towards a deterministic order.

Summary

Complexity can be identified in schooling and teaching systems. Each school, region, department, and network of teachers has the characteristics of a complex system with unique variables or parts such as its history, culture, community, leadership, students, policies, communication networks, structures, resources and teachers. Knowledge emerges as new and diverse ideas, resources, processes, events or practices are introduced. During the process some existing beliefs, policies or practices are modified and some may become redundant. It is through this process of diversity and redundancy, controlled collectively by the parts of the system (influenced by historical experiences), that new knowledge emerges which will be unique in some way to the complex system. Teaching and learning in the digital age is considered in the following chapters through a complexity theory perspective.

Chapter 2

The digital age

As societies become more complex in structure and resources, the need of formal or intentional teaching and learning increases.

(Dewey, 1916, p. 255)

Societies change over time through events, innovations and evolving ideologies. The introduction of digital technologies and related infrastructure could signify the commencement of social change at a similar scale to that experienced during and following the industrial revolution. Like the industrial age, a digital age is a time of innovations and inventions which act as catalysts for change within complex systems on the macro level (national or global) and the micro level (small complex organisations such as schools). This chapter explores how innovations and societal change can influence education using the industrial age as a point of reference for considering teaching and learning in the digital age.

The industrial age

During the industrial age there were a series of related innovations which significantly altered how many communities, nations and societies functioned and interacted. Changes to transport, communication, social and economic processes occurred over decades as the complex systems within society evolved. The development of manufacturing industries were connected to a range of social changes that influenced how teaching and learning was conceptualised. Industrialising countries and many of their colonies had introduced policies aimed at increasing universal participation in schooling by the end of the industrial age.

The development of steam power increased transportation speed and capacity within and between nations, meeting the increasing demand for traded materials during the industrial age. The industries that developed needed raw materials which were not always available locally. Having the reliability of a colonial source of supply contributed to the expansion of empires, growth of nationalism and potential conflict. Social structures were affected by the industrialisation. Urbanisation occurred as farm and rural employment opportunities were fewer than those seeking work and workers were attracted to the opportunities offered in rapidly growing towns or cities. The migration of people and growth of industries changed the complex organisations of industrialising societies.

The development of factories and industries coincided with the beginning of mass publication of written materials. The steam-powered rotary press replaced the earlier Guttenberg press, enabling books to be printed on an industrial scale thus increasing the access of written knowledge beyond the clergy, academics and the wealthy, to anyone who was able to read and gain copies of books. By the end of the industrial revolution mass schooling was seen as a way of achieving literate and patriotic nations with the knowledge to continue to advance society. This is reflected in the writing of John Dewey who believed it was important for everyone in a democratic society to be able to understand symbols and text. He was a proponent of universal access to schooling so that the following generation could learn what the previous generation knew:

> as civilization advances ... [the] ability to share effectively in adult activities thus depends upon a prior training given. With this end in view intentional agencies – schools – and explicit material – studies – are devised. The task of teaching certain things is delegated to a special group of persons ... Without such formal education, it is not possible to transmit all the resources and achievements of a complex society.
>
> (Dewey, 1916)

From Dewey's perspective the purpose of school was to ensure that society did not regress to barbarism; he believed that the next generation could not learn through an apprentice/mentoring model (he noted that this was what 'savages' used), but needed to master the 'symbols of knowledge' (reading, writing and arithmetic). This infers that teachers had an important role in advancing societal knowledge. He advocated for everyone in society to gain this knowledge through schooling and have a voice in society. The process of, and ideas about, education for children was an aspect of society that evolved during the industrial age with schooling for the masses becoming policy in a number of countries.

It appears that a number of nations were achieving high levels of enrolment at primary schools by the end of the industrial age. The Argyll Commission investigated the state of education in Scotland in 1864–67 and reported that 418,000 of the 510,000 (81 per cent) 4- to 14-year-old Scottish children were enrolled in school (Connell, 1980). The commission also reported favourably high enrolment rates for high school when compared with other countries (Table 2.1).

The aim of schooling is and has been to prepare young people to contribute to society. In the industrial age this meant preparing the young people to work in industry, to produce or attain the materials needed for industry or society (through farming or trade), protect or increase the advantages that the society has (be prepared to fight for the country), develop economic competitive advantage and keep the social fabric of the community operating and patriotic. National or state curriculum was developed in the industrial age with these aims in mind. Schools included pathways that channelled young people towards their

Table 2.1 Enrolment at high school, selected countries in 1867

Country (1867)	Ratio of young people enrolled in high school
Scotland	1:205
England	1:1300
France	1:1500
Prussia	1:249

Source: Connell, 1980.

contribution to society. Besides learning reading, writing and arithmetic and learning nationalistic values, some students were expected to become mothers and housewives, therefore curriculum included home economics, sewing and health. Others were to join the trades, farm or be unskilled workers and be prepared to fight for their country. Their curriculum included woodwork, crafts, military training and physical education. Those who stayed in education for more than six years were more likely to become government workers, teachers, bankers and white collar workers or the knowledge producers of the future, the academics, leaders and the clergy, who were taught the classics, literature, geography and history.

While the aim of education remains to prepare young people to contribute to society, the interpretation of what this means is debated. There are differing perspectives about the relative importance of the social versus the economic preparation that should be included in curriculum, and within each of these there are differing perspectives.

The cultural context of a nation influenced educational policies and priorities. The Scottish Argyll commission report expressed disdain for the English system that restricted education of the labouring classes to the basics (McDermid, 2006); instead it wanted to see talented boys, regardless of their father's status, have the opportunity to schooling beyond primary school. The Scottish Education Act, 1872 made parents responsible for ensuring their children were taught reading, writing and arithmetic. If the parents could not afford fees, the Act allowed for application to school boards for remission of fees, and any person who employed a child under 13 years was held in loco parentis, subject to the same penalties as the parents if the child could not read or write (Scotland, 1969).

The Japanese government introduced a national education framework in an effort to match the powers of the industrialised nations (or empires) in the same year as the Scottish Education Act of 1872. One of the aims was to strengthen the family and imperial loyalties (Connell, 1980). From 1900 Japanese secondary school enrolments escalated at a pace comparable to industrial growth. These examples illustrate how contexts are connected yet each is unique in the detail of organisational systemic change. Complexity theory can provide a framework to consider how education systems evolved in the industrial age, and Figure 2.1 provides a simplified model as an example.

Aspects of complex societies such as school curriculum development can be considered using the complexity theory outlined in Chapter 1. The evolution of curriculum development from the teaching and learning perspective are unpredictable. The context of curriculum change is usually a national context, where the developers involved may include lobby groups, university academics, publishers, teachers, teaching associations and government employees. There is likely to be a cultural context to the way that the decisions are made which builds on historical experience. Mark Sheehan (2010) explored how History curriculum decisions were made in 1980s New Zealand and found that those making the decisions sometimes had a narrow perspective based on their own interests rather than a national perspective.

The innovations or change catalysts that inspire curriculum development can include political change, emerging academic or pedagogical knowledge from within the nation or from examining what other nations are doing (particularly those who are scoring higher on international tests such as PISA). The structures within a national education system include levels from the teachers in classes to the Ministry of Education, as with schools these are ambiguously bound and there are many connected levels. The development process will include examining a diversity of possibilities for curriculum and making a number of

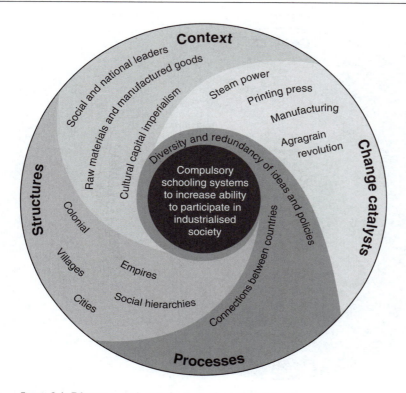

Figure 2.1 Education and complexity in the industrial age.

curriculum ideas redundant (Figure 2.2). It should be noted that just because a curriculum changes it does not mean that changes to teaching and learning within a classroom context will occur. This is the complexity of educational change.

By the end of the 1800s the first cars were appearing, electricity was being explored and the telephone had been developed. It is not predictable how innovations will change society. The first cars were developed from the idea of carriages without horses and were slow, expensive and problematic to use. Few people would have seen the future of such an innovation. Bill Bryson (2010) explains that when the telephone was invented it attracted very little attention as it was unclear to people why they would want to have this sort of social interaction rather than a face-to-face exchange.

From a complexity theorist's perspective the industrial age did not have a defining starting point or end point. It included a series of innovations such as harnessing the energy from coal to produce power, the mass production of goods and agricultural reform. These and the numerous other innovations altered how communities, nations, and societies functioned, interacted and perceived themselves and others. The development of industries had a significant and ongoing global influence including the growth of imperialism, complex economic structures, knowledge sharing and the release of greenhouse gases into the atmosphere. It was within this context of urbanisation changing work patterns and the increasing availability of the written word that universal schooling emerged; the nature and detail of this varied according to the cultural context and the time.

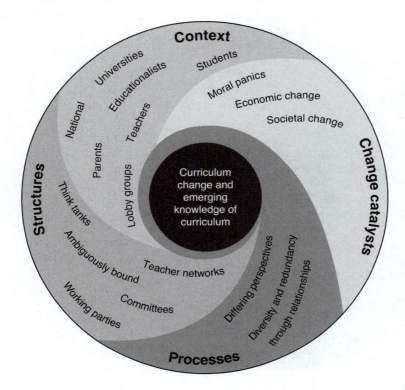

Figure 2.2 Complexity and evolving curricular.

The digital age

The development of digital technologies and supporting infrastructure could herald the beginning of a 'digital age'. Like the industrial age, there have been a series of related innovations which appear to be significantly altering how communities, nations and societies function and interact. The changes and innovations are likely to continue to occur over decades and the complex systems within society will evolve.

The innovations that have emerged at the start of the digital age include home computing, the World Wide Web, online social networks, mobile or wireless capability, and communication technologies. Each is underpinned by numerous inventions. This sample of innovations may not be the most significant in the digital age but they are a selection which is influencing society from the community to the global level.

Mobile phone technologies have influenced how families and friends communicate. Ten group interviews were undertaken in 1999 in Norway to gather information on the way that teenagers used cell phones. Ling and Yttri (2002) found that cell phones were used for micro-coordination: organising meetings, transport arrangements and so forth with family and friends. The introduction of mobile technology to the family and social groups has seen this ability to keep in regular easy contact, to arrange when and where to meet, and send messages such as what is needed from the supermarket. This has changed the way that families can operate in that all arrangements do not need to be made during face-to-face contact prior to the start of time away from each other, which could increase flexibility with time and alter the dynamics of family organisational processes. This is an example of how the introduction of digital technologies to societies changes the way communities or groups operate.

Social networking is also subtly changing how families and friends connect and communicate. Through social networking sites groups stay in contact, acquaintances remain, photographs shared and trivial and important personal news can be shared immediately and widely. It would be interesting to compare the pre-industrial age communication patterns of people living in small communities with people today in the digital age who are connected with their friends and acquaintances through social networking.

Digital technologies have infiltrated the lives of young people through the use of interactive programmes designed for preschoolers, children and youth, gaming and mobile communication devices. Young people join social networks where they share information online, take part in online gaming, upload and share creative endeavours, and are in constant contact with peers through mobile technologies.

There has been research interest in how youth as a subset of societies operate within the digital age. There is no evidence that the current generation of students' brains are wired differently or that they are less able to concentrate than previous generations. In a 2006 study of 935 12- to 17-year-olds and their parents in the USA, Lenhart *et al.* (2007) found that 93 per cent of the teens surveyed were using the Internet with increasing numbers using interacting through the World Wide Web. This included 39 per cent of online teens sharing their artistic creations online (artwork, photos, stories, or videos), 28 per cent blogging, and 26 per cent mashing content they found online into their own creations. These figures show an increase from an earlier similar survey taken in 2004 (Lenhart and Madden, 2005), which found teenagers accessing tools to remix and create media, and half of the teenagers in the study were found to be content creators, blogging, remixing, or creating their own digital products. Analysis of the same data set found that 89 per cent of the teens thought that digital technologies made their life easier (Macgill, 2007).

Research from Australia examined university students' use of digital technologies and found both diversity and uniformity. The university students relied heavily on digital technologies for study, listening to music, for keeping in touch with friends through calling and texting, and for information gathering (Kennedy *et al.*, 2008). In a 2005 study of children from the United Kingdom, four categories of digital technology users were identified: digital pioneers, creative producers, everyday communicators and information gatherers (Green and Hannon, 2007). These results reflect some diversity amongst users and the report acknowledged that not all young people are digital *enthusiasts*, despite the ubiquitous use of cell phones and digital music players.

It can be assumed that young people today in most nations will be familiar with the Internet, be diverse in their attitudes to digital technologies, and that the majority own a digital device to keep in touch frequently with friends and family. Some will be connecting online for gaming, instant chat or social networking, finding information, downloading music or sharing creative products with others.

The ability to connect remotely in the digital age has the potential to change processes within and across complex organisation on a global scale. Online gaming is an example of an innovation the implications of which are unknown and unpredictable. Currently people with broadband access and an interest in online gaming (typically boys or young men) collaborate in simulated battles. They meet other players whose progress they are able to follow and they are able to invite them into games, along with their local friends. The community members teach each other how to achieve higher scores through synchronous online chat or messaging. Members develop movie tutorials and share these online through social networks or sites such as YouTube. This is an example of how global networks develop in the digital age.

Global significance

A significant innovation in the digital age is the World Wide Web. Being able to connect internationally to synchronously talk, video conference, collaboratively develop concepts or reports, and engage in commercial interactions could change economics and the operation of businesses. The global context could be perceived as one large complex market with many levels. This may have begun prior to the digital age with multinational corporations, but is likely to develop at many different scales through the World Wide Web. Early examples include the introduction of online shopping, outsourcing of businesses, and electronic books. The global significance will not be limited to the way that commercial enterprises operate, but will also influence how nations develop, interact, and respond to each other and events.

Tapscott and Williams (2006) focus on the way that people participate in the market by using *weapons of mass collaboration* (social networking). In their book *Wikinomics* they explore and speculate what happens when groups of people and organisations collaborate openly to drive innovation and growth in their industries. They note that people can be producers rather than just consumers of information and ideas, and some global entities such as the pharmaceutical industry, marketing, and scientific organisations are using this to boost their knowledge base and potentiate innovations. The idea that access to the Internet can result in individuals collectively contributing to the global knowledge base has implications for schooling and pedagogical beliefs, which will be explored in Chapter 3.

In the digital age it is no longer necessary for many workers to attend a common workplace each day. In some professions it is possible to live on a different continent and fully participate in an organisation without ever being in the same room as your colleagues. This ability to work from a remote location offers choice and allows companies to make use of expertise without having to relocate families. When complex organisations choose to give employees the option of working remotely a number of processes, policies and communication structures will evolve across all levels of the system. An interesting comparison could be made with the industrial age when people had to move to where they could participate in work.

The potential for individuals to collaborate through global connections available through digital technology and the Internet is enabling geographically diverse people to form like-minded groups. Anderson (2006) examined the impact of the Internet on sales and marketing of products which would not be viable in a small geographically bound community. He found that in a global community the market for special interest products such as a particular type of music or book can become profitable and accessible, hence the success of Amazon and eBay. He called this phenomenon 'the long tail'. The idea of the long tail can be applied to the educational context. Through the World Wide Web, learners and knowledge creators are able to connect globally with other learners with similar interests, to collaborate and critique.

Teaching and learning or schooling is part of society and therefore likely to evolve during the digital age, as it did during the industrial age. There has been some consideration about teaching and learning with digital technologies with researchers exploring responses to the introduction of digital technologies within schools.

As part of a doctoral thesis, Brown (2004) examined the use of computers in schools and developed a metaphor for the changes over time. He identified four waves of computer use in schools, each wave washing over the previous one, with teachers jumping onto the wave to ride with it. The four waves he identified included:

- the instructional wave (1975–85) – the computer was the instructional tutor;
- the problem solving wave (1980–90) – students teach the computer;
- the mind tool wave (1985–95) – the computer is a tool;
- the media wave (1995–2004) – learning from the information available on the Internet.

During the instructional, problem solving and mind tool waves, which were prior to the widespread use of the Internet, digital technologies were used within specific subject areas, particularly in mathematics, science and computing. The mind tool wave teachers were starting to use presentation software as a teaching tool. The media wave saw the introduction of access to information through the Internet in schools and hence inquiry learning with differing degrees of teacher control over the content and direction. The wave model was presented in 2004 so therefore did not include social networking or the use of digital technologies to connect beyond the classroom environment.

Schools have been accumulating digital technologies since the 1990s and the focus in the literature has turned to examine how teachers are using these digital technologies in their teaching practice and the outcomes for students. Four different categories of the use of digital technologies in schools emerge from the literature: subject specific interactive uses, presentation of information, accessing information and connecting online.

The first use is one of using particular programmes and technologies for specific purposes within subjects. This aligns with what Brown (2004) called the problem solving wave, the instructional wave and mind tool wave. Examples include the use of Logo in mathematics or technology, and simulation activities in the social sciences.

The second use is the use of technologies to present information, ideas and concepts. This includes teachers developing paper-based resources using word processing software in the 1980s and including PowerPoint presentations and Internet-based information and multimedia presentations through a data show or interactive whiteboard since 2000. In a study of 39 schools in England it was found the main use of digital technologies in the English schools was word processing, presentations and accessing information from the Internet (Ofsted, 2005).

In a study of New Zealand teachers' use of laptops, it was found that at the end of 2005 60 per cent used their laptops with data projectors and the most prevalent use of the laptop and peripherals was to present visual material as part of the instruction to the class (Cowie et al., 2008). Teachers who used their laptops during lessons to present multi-media materials reported that this engaged students creatively and critically in their learning. Having the teacher presenting multimedia materials to the class can be a transmission approach to teaching. Students are likely to find the range of visual media more engaging than listening to a teacher standing by a board and talking or writing notes to be copied.

The third use resulted from increasing availability and reliability of information through the Internet, which coincided with a growing trend towards the use of inquiry-based learning, particularly in the social sciences and sciences in secondary school. This is the time that Brown described as the media wave. Digital technologies have been used by students to access information from national and international organisations or publishers to use as a basis for an inquiry learning project. Experienced teachers who are introducing digital technology alongside their existing teaching practice have been found to be impressed when students use presentation software or other ways of using digital technologies which require minimal cognitive engagement by students (Clifford *et al.*, 2005). Where a teacher previously asked students to create a poster that pulls together information gathered from books, they may now ask the student to print off a presentation using online sources. Instead of copying drawings and hand-writing paragraphs they cut and paste and use fonts, Word Art and other software to make the output look impressive. If the teacher focused on the content and presentation of the finished product and not the learning or the process, they were likely to be impressed. This finding illustrates that the teacher's pedagogical beliefs did not change even though their teaching practice altered to include student use of digital technologies.

The fourth use of digital technologies in schools is to make connections across geographical spaces, between information sources, media and ideas. There are fewer examples of this in the literature. A challenge identified in a harnessing technology review (Becta, 2007) was developing the use of technology from enhancing and enriching learning to also extending and empowering it, and developing a broader repertoire of practitioner skills.

A second area of research at the start of the digital age is from a policy and funding perspective, exploring the influence of digital technologies on learning. Towards the end of the 1990s a growing tension about the value of using computers in schools is found in the literature. The policy and assumptions about the benefits of computers in schools was being questioned by educational writers such as Oppenheimer (1997) and Cuban (2001).

Oppenheimer (1997) expressed concern at the US government's desire to increase computer ratios and computer use in schools at the expense of learning arts and physical education. He noted that research which reported improved student achievement and innovative use of computer were anecdotal rather than research based and that it was the teachers' pedagogical approach that was behind improved student learning rather than the use of the digital technologies.

Cuban (2001) noted that the teachers in his study adapted computer use to fit with their traditional practices rather than adapting the way they teach to take account of the opportunities offered by computers (as had been hoped by policy makers and some proponents of information communication technologies). When he considered the introduction of computers in schools with previous innovations, he found that the process of change in schools can be intergenerational, taking decades rather than a few months or years. Research in the early 2000s tended to focus on *if* teachers were using digital technologies in their teaching and the factors that were helping or preventing their use of them.

There is an evolving range of literature since the introduction of digital technologies into secondary schools. Cox *et al.* (2004) reviewed studies on the use of digital technologies and student attainment and concluded that digital technologies only enhance student achievement when it is combined with effective teaching practices. This review reflected the emerging focus in the literature on how aspects of secondary schooling impact on student learning, in this case how digital technologies are being used to enhance student learning. It is clearly the teaching and the teachers rather than the use of specific technologies that will be the most influential aspect of learning in digital age schools.

Summary

The industrial age was an era of social change that may be compared to the significance of change expected in the digital age. During the industrial age compulsory schooling was introduced in a number of nations to enable participation in society of a literate, numerate and patriotic population.

The introduction of digital technologies to society has the potential to significantly change how societies function. The use of networked mobile devices enables social networking, instant communication, micromanagement of social engagements, and access to information and data from any location. These influence how aspects of society operate on an individual to global scale.

Digital technologies are being used in schools and have been since the 1980s. Their uses and functions have slowly changed over time and have been influenced by the technologies available, pedagogical beliefs, practices, schooling structures, and policies. The influence of digital technologies on teaching and learning reflects the complexity of the schooling system and how it is intertwined with the broader context of society. The purpose of schooling has been, and continues to be, to educate each generation to participate effectively in society. Therefore education policies and practices will evolve as society evolves. The changes within teaching and learning within the digital age is likely to be a relatively slow process, over a time span of decades.

Chapter 3

Knowledge and connectivism

The introduction of new ideas and innovations can alter structures, hierarchies, and roles within and across communities. How knowledge is perceived, developed and controlled may evolve through systemic societal change. The introduction of digital technologies to society is influencing ideas about knowledge and learning theory, and beliefs about teaching and learning in the digital age.

Perspectives of knowledge

Dewey (1916) suggested that the purpose of schools is to develop educated individuals or cohorts to actively participate in society. Globally this continues to be the primary purpose of schooling, although what it means to participate in society can vary between contexts and over time. In the industrial age it appears that participation was through being literate, numerate, patriotic, and having a general knowledge of what was known about how society functioned in the present and the past. Perspectives on participation in society influence educational policy decisions about curriculum development, school structures and pedagogy. Such perspectives are underpinned by economic, cultural and epistemological beliefs and values. It is the epistemological beliefs or understandings of the nature of knowledge that is of particular interest when considering teaching and learning in the digital age. How and where knowledge is conceived to be developed influences policies, learning theories and teaching decisions.

Epistemological perspectives vary over time and between educationalists. Questions of how and where knowledge is developed, and how knowledge is shared, underpin learning theories and the essence of schooling structures and practices. Educational researchers study, debate and collaboratively develop learning theory by examining past and present complexities of schooling including policies, student learning and teaching. The explicit and implicit perspectives of educational researchers about knowledge influence theories of learning and ultimately teacher education programmes and teaching and learning processes within schools.

Policy makers examine research findings as they develop policies which influence curriculum, funding, systems and structures. The aim of national schooling policies is the goal of having school leavers able to participate in society. While a national or state curriculum may mandate teaching content, resources, pedagogies and age related achievement targets, it is teachers that individually and collectively make professional decisions about how they will teach the students in their classes. John Hattie undertook a meta-analysis that calculated the effect sizes of various aspects of schooling and found that teachers have the greatest effect on student learning and achievement (Hattie, 2009). Teaching decisions are an important influence on how well individuals or cohorts are prepared to participate in society as they leave the schooling system.

Figure 3.1 illustrates the relationship between knowledge and the schooling system. The dominant epistemological beliefs of the time (perspective of knowledge) underpin the learning theory which influences teaching decisions. Teaching decisions determine student learning, and what a generation of students learn at school will influence how they participate in society when they leave school. The policy makers consider school leavers' participation in society and the work of the educational researchers, the educational researchers examine the different aspects, share findings with the sector, and contribute to the development of learning theory.

How knowledge develops is complex and can be viewed in different ways. Prior to the industrial age societies had people who were responsible for specific areas of knowledge and passing it on to the next generation. These included spiritual leaders, skilled craftsmen and women, tribal, village or regional leaders and philosophers or early academics. In some societies aspects of knowledge were recorded in a written format. Knowledge was shared through story telling, metaphors, modelling, apprenticing and tutoring.

In the industrial age formal schooling began to become a global phenomenon. Certain types of knowledge were identified as being important to meet the political and economic aims of society. National or regional curriculum evolved based on those aims and influenced what was to be taught within a schooling system. This was at a time that a positivist epistemological perspective of knowledge dominated.

Schooling in the industrial age was underpinned by a positivist perspective of knowledge which meant that academics and scientists sought to examine and understand the world as a god had created it. Learning the truth was essential to the development of societal knowledge and society itself. A positivist perspective of knowledge meant that once something

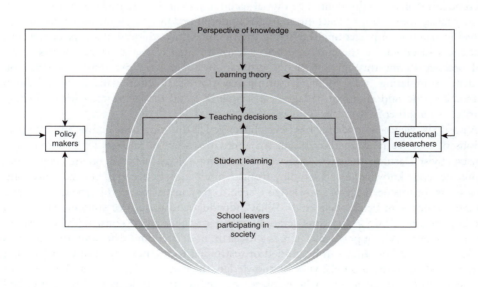

Figure 3.1 The relationship between epistemology and schooling.

was proven through empirical scientific inquiry, it was considered to be factual or the truth. When this knowledge was considered important for everyone to know it may be included in the school curriculum to be learnt by all young people. This was seen as how society was to advance and is reflected in the literature by authors such as Dewey (1900).

Knowledge and learning theories

The behaviourist learning theory emerged from a positivist perspective of knowledge where learning is the acquisition of new behaviour. A teaching strategy commonly associated with this theory is 'direct instruction', where teachers tell students, present them with the 'truth' through speaking, showing, or modelling, students learn this knowledge without critiquing it, then demonstrate what they have learnt through reflecting back the same knowledge as they have been taught in an assessment task such as a test or exam. A teacher's perspective of their responsibilities included ensuring that they taught the prescribed knowledge. Behaviourist teaching strategies include focusing on ensuring all students have recorded the correct notes into their work books or portfolios.

A curriculum underpinned by a positivist perspective of knowledge is an outcomes based curriculum with specific prescribed knowledge and skills to be taught. Bloom's taxonomy was a useful pedagogical aid for teaching and learning, strongly reflecting the positive perspective of knowledge. Bloom's affective domain ties learning with behavioural learning theory. The highest level in this domain is *characterising*, which was defined as *where the student holds a particular value or belief that exerts influence on his/her behaviour so that it becomes a characteristic* (Bloom *et al.*, 1956). In Bloom's cognitive domain *knowledge* was the lowest level of learning. Students were conceived as empty vessels waiting to have their minds filled with important knowledge passed on by their teacher and through their academic study (Figure 3.2).

The digital age does not mean that the positivist or behaviourist view of knowledge will become immediately redundant. The digital technologies and tools available at the start of the digital age can reinforce teaching strategies underpinned by behaviourist learning theory. Direct instruction or presenting the 'truth' can be done through multimedia presentations. Students can download the correct notes to learn through learning management systems and practice exams through interactive programmes. Teaching can remain focused on students completing tasks. While lecturing may not be the dominant mode of direct instruction, the underpinning pedagogical strategies could remain aligned with a behaviourist learning theory from the industrial age.

A positivist view of knowledge has been challenged as differing perspectives and interpretations of 'the truth' were recognised. An alternative view of knowledge underpins the constructivist learning theories. Constructivist epistemology is based on the belief that people generate knowledge and meaning from an interaction between their experiences and their ideas. In this perspective knowledge is seen to be constructed within the heads of the learners rather than being 'delivered'. What individual and groups of students know and perceive becomes important considerations when teachers apply constructivist learning theory to their teaching practice. There is a focus on understanding what and how students are learning, and how they can be guided or scaffolded to the next stage of their learning (Figure 3.3). Like the positivist view of knowledge, the constructivist view also aligns with an outcomes based curriculum where the teacher guides the students towards prescribed outcomes that are assessed to evaluate the successfulness of the teaching and the learning.

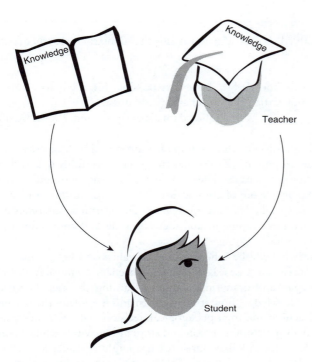

Figure 3.2 Positivist perspective.

Figure 3.3 Constructivist perspective.

Scardamalia and Bereiter (2006) noted a paradox in the constructivist theory of learning:

> If learners construct their own knowledge, how is it possible for them to create a cognitive structure more complex than the one they already possess?
>
> (Scardamalia and Bereiter, 2006, p. 103)

Educators commonly answer this question by drawing on ideas proposed by Vygotsky, who suggested a 'zone of proximal development' (ZPD) that the teacher scaffolds the student through during language acquisition processes. The ZPD being the gap between what is already known or mastered to the next stage of complexity. Thus the role of the teacher is to guide the students towards the specific learning outcomes. The learning outcomes are commonly identified within curriculum documents and focus on skills and knowledge that will help participation in society as adults.

A teacher's beliefs about knowledge will be reflected in their values and beliefs and will influence the way they express their successes as a teacher. Teachers commonly switch between different teaching strategies and draw on a range of learning theories, however their core values and beliefs about knowledge, how students learn and the role of the teacher will influence the goals of their teaching and their pedagogical decision making. A positivist will fundamentally focus on the delivery of information and student behaviour while a constructivist will focus on student learning. A behaviourist teacher might consider himself or herself successful when their students have a full set of tidy notes, pay attention in class, respond with the expected answers to questions, and develop a passion for the subject or content being taught. A constructivist would express satisfaction when their students have demonstrated individual improvement in their understanding of subject knowledge and confidence in applying the skills.

A third view of knowledge is emerging in the digital age. In 2002 Carl Bereiter called for a new way of thinking about knowledge and the mind. He advocated a move away from the idea of the mind as a container which he saw as a 'two-dimensional world of folk theory' (p. 461) to a three-dimensional world better suited to the digital age. Jane Gilbert (2005) suggests that knowledge should be a verb rather than a noun. Both authors point to the importance of collaboration and connections in the knowledge building process.

Learners in the digital age are able connect and collaborate with people beyond their physical environment. They can connect a range of information or data and draw on a range of perspectives to collaboratively generate and critique new ideas. Both Gilbert (2005) and Bereiter (2002) note the distinction between learning and creating knowledge. George Siemens (2006) explores this further, noting that to learn 'is to come to know. To know is to have learned. We seek knowledge so that we can make sense' (p. 26). Learning involves developing understanding of concepts or skills whereas knowledge development involves connecting information, ideas or processes in new ways.

In the digital age the abundance of information and ideas available at an individual's fingertips through the Internet is phenomenal when compared with access in the industrial age. Social networking and the interactive web enable anyone with Internet access to not only find information, but to interact, present their own ideas, make connections and collaborate through self-selected networks. Thus knowledge is becoming decentralised. Complexity theory and ideas emerging from the digital age have contributed to rethinking about the way that knowledge is conceptualised (Siemens, 2006). Knowledge is constantly being created, shared and reviewed and this occurs through connections between people and information sources. This view of knowledge is different to positivist and constructivist perspectives. While creating knowledge continues to be about understanding why the world is as it is, it can also be about how it could be and the 'what if' questions. It is not focused on finding a truth as there are different ways to interpret information or to view a problem or scenario. It includes deconstructing as well as constructing ideas collaboratively. Knowledge is developed not in the heads of individuals, but between people and sources of information (Figure 3.4).

An example of this view of knowledge which is derived from complexity theory can be drawn from the creation of knowledge within educational research. The understanding of how digital technologies can and will influence teaching and learning within schools has evolved over the past 30 years. This knowledge has evolved at many levels including the teacher in the classroom who learns from his or her students and shares this with colleagues to develop a shared understanding. Researchers have examined how the use of digital technologies impacts on learning using data from a significant number of schools. The findings are shared with the global research community where they are critiqued and reinterpreted by differing researcher and practitioner perspectives. These levels are not isolated and the evolved knowledge occurs through the discussions and debate. It is through the connections between the people and information that new knowledge emerges. This can be through communities of practice, classrooms, teaching or research publications, online forums, formal and informal learning networks.

Diversity and redundancy of ideas occur as knowledge is constructed and deconstructed. One example of this is the development of the concept of 'technological pedagogical

Figure 3.4 Connectivist perspective.

content knowledge' (Mishra and Koehler, 2008). How digital technologies can be used to teach particular subject based concepts and skills may be an important aspect of teacher knowledge at the start of a digital age, however, this idea is likely to become redundant and subsumed into pedagogical content knowledge as the use of digital technologies within teaching becomes normalised.

There is randomness and deterministic order in the creation of knowledge. The types and use of digital technologies in schools may appear to be random and unpredictable (what will teachers and students be using in 20 years time?); however, there is deterministic order as the purpose of schooling, learning and teaching tends to underpin the emerging knowledge. The deterministic order is influenced by the history, culture and values of the teaching profession and communities in which they operate.

Connectivist learning theory

Ideas about knowledge underpin learning theory and pedagogical practice and therefore influence teaching and learning in schools. George Siemens developed 'connectivism' as a learning theory for the digital era. Connectivism aims to provide a theory that considers how people, organisations and technology can collaboratively construct knowledge. The theory builds on ideas that have emerged since the introduction of widespread interaction and access to information through the Internet and is underpinned by complexity theory. Siemens (2004) describes connectivism as:

> The integration of principles explored by chaos, network, and complexity and self-organization theories. Learning is a process that occurs within nebulous environments of shifting core elements – not entirely under the control of the individual. Learning (defined as actionable knowledge) can reside outside of ourselves (within an organization or a database), is focused on connecting specialized information sets, and the connections that enable us to learn more are more important than our current state of knowing.
>
> (paragraph 21)

A learning theory for the digital age should consider learning as a continual process within a complex environment rather than an event. A central idea in the learning theory of connectivism is the continual expansion of knowledge as new and novel connections open new interpretations and understandings to create new knowledge.

Connectivist learning theory has itself been discussed through digitised connections. The theory has evolved in the blogosphere with a variety of educationalists interacting through open online networks to discuss and debate the theory, which has in turn, contributed to its development.

Curriculum

If participation in society in the future includes citizens actively involved in the development of knowledge then policy makers will include learning to create knowledge in school curricular. Such curricular would need flexibility and not be restrained by the current outcomes approach. This would have implications for not only pedagogical approaches but also the

	Conceptions of learning	Pedagogical approaches to teaching and learning	Learning and developing knowledge and skills	Participation in society
Industrial age:	Giving knowledge, passing on what is known.	Telling, showing, testing. Outcomes based pedagogy and curriculum.	Constructing knowledge and skills.	Educated, patriotic, obedient, critical, literate and numerate.
Digital age:	Knowledge is debatable, develops through connections, open to be developed and critiqued.	Students collaborating beyond the classroom context, critical, creative. Flexible outcomes developed from core concepts.	Collaborating, developing conceptual understanding, creating and critiquing knowledge, making and maintaining connections.	Connected, critical, creative, actively developing knowledge.
Focus of:	Educational researchers/theorists	Teachers	Learners	Education policy makers

Figure 3.5 Comparison of knowledge and teaching in the digital and industrial ages.

structures within schools. The assessment of learning would evolve to be appropriate to the curriculum intentions.

A curriculum for learning in the digital age will continue to include concepts that will help each generation understand the world in which they live and the skills to participate in society. Each subject will continue to have core concepts and skills which students will need to understand as part of their education; these may change as knowledge within the subject domain evolves. The exact nature of the changes are not predictable due to the complexity of how societies evolve.

Concepts and skills included in curriculum undergo the process outlined in complexity theory as redundancy and diversity. For example essay writing is a skill which may become redundant in the digital age (and it may not). The presentation of information is becoming less linear (as seen in an essay) and increasingly three-dimensional, with hyperlinks or navigation within and across key ideas or concepts. This is occurring at a time that people when they access information may not start at the beginning and work through to the end and may surf around to find what they are seeking to understand. It could be that in the digital age arguments, concepts and information are presented and viewed in ways that are different to a sequential essay and the skill of essay writing begins to be redundant. Such a change is not unprecedented. The ability to accurately recall lineages or stories became redundant, or less widely known, when the written word became the preferred way of recording societal knowledge. If essay writing is a skill that does become redundant there are likely to be other skills that are deemed to be important in the digital age that will be taught as a means of expressing understanding of concepts. New skills and conceptual understandings will be taught and learnt in the schooling sector as part of the diversity experienced as the complex system evolves.

Summary

How knowledge is viewed changes over time and between contexts. In educational theory two perspectives of knowledge have dominated beliefs about teaching and learning. One reflects a positivist view of knowledge and was dominant in the industrial age and the second is from a constructivist perspective. In the digital age knowledge can be considered from a third perspective underpinned by complexity theory. Such a view of knowledge includes the following characteristics:

- Knowledge is created by connecting information, ideas and processes in new ways
- Knowledge is created through connections between people and/or technologies
- Knowledge can be considered from different perspectives
- Knowledge is continually expanding

Learning theory is underpinned by epistemological beliefs and as ideas about knowledge evolve learning theories also evolve. A positivist view of knowledge can be associated with behaviourist and constructivist learning theories. Connectivism learning theory is emerging from a complexity theoretical perspective of knowledge. The pedagogical approaches of teachers are underpinned by their beliefs about knowledge and their application of learning theory. Therefore perspectives of knowledge and learning theory will continue to influence teaching and learning in the digital age.

Chapter 4

Connections and relationships

Teaching and learning in the digital age is likely to be underpinned by connectivist learning theory which has emerged from a decentralised view of knowledge based on complexity. Complexity theory proposes that the emergence of knowledge occurs through the connections between the parts or participants within and beyond a system. At the heart of complexity theory are the interactions between the connected parts of a system or organisation including relationships through which the agency and mutual influence of individuals and groups create a responsive process. In a schooling context the responsive process includes the process of teaching and learning.

Connectivist learning theory asserts that knowledge is created through connections and learning occurs through the networks to which learners belong. Teachers in the digital age encourage the development of connections for the purpose of learning with and between their students, their community, other learners, experts beyond the classroom, and to make connections between experiences and knowledge as part of the learning process.

Teacher–student connection

Pedagogical practice in the digital age includes the active development of learning relationships which may have been perceived as less necessary when the purpose of schooling was perceived from a positivist perspective as imparting important knowledge from the voice of authority (the teacher and texts) to the passive learner (the student). Marzano (2000) carried out a meta-analysis on aspects that affect student achievement and noted that a teacher has a significant effect on student achievement. Using a different approach, John Hattie (2009) synthesised over 800 meta-analysis to summarise the effect size of various aspects of teaching, context and curricula on outcomes based learning. He concluded that the teacher has the greatest influence on student achievement; what they do, how they teach matters. If it is a teacher's job to teach it is their moral responsibility to ensure that their students are learning.

The connection between the teacher and the student is a significant component in the teaching and learning process. The teacher designs learning activities to teach and explore key concepts or skills based on curriculum requirements, pedagogical content knowledge, the students' learning needs and experiences, resources and the context in which the learning will occur. This requires the teacher to be a skilled professional with an understanding of curriculum, concepts and skills to be taught, pedagogical approaches, the context in which the learners will learn, and the learners themselves. They need to be able to establish and maintain an effective learning environment where students feel safe, empowered to collaborate, ask questions, ask for help with their learning, discuss their learning with their teacher, and to take risks like putting forward their ideas which may be different to the teachers or other learners in the group. To establish and maintain an effective learning environment a teacher needs to develop a positive and responsive relationship with his or her students. Establishing and maintaining a positive teacher–student learning relationship is the responsibility of the teacher. It is an important component of effective teaching.

The relationship teachers have with their students has been studied and recognised as important. Cornelius-White (2007) carried out a meta-analysis of 119 studies to explore the effect student centred teaching has on learning. He correlated nine teacher variables with positive student outcomes and found that four of his variables had a strong positive correlation with an effect size above 0.5 including being nondirective, empathetic, warm and encouraging thinking. Each of these variables can contribute to a positive teacher–student learning relationship.

Students have prior experience of learning and being a learner before being placed with a particular teacher. The student brings knowledge, experiences and values to the learning relationship which extends beyond curriculum based learning and influences how they approach the relationship and the expectations they have of 'teachers' and what learning involves.

Te Kotahitanga was an initiative to improve academic achievement for Maori students. As part of this initiative researchers asked 70 Maori students about their experience in New Zealand schools. An important aspect identified by the students was the relationship they had with their teacher:

> The discussions about the importance of relationships not only emphasised how important it was for Maori students to see that their teachers cared for them as Maori people but that this caring relationship also meant that teachers were concerned to develop a learning relationship with the students.
>
> (Bishop and Berryman, 2006, p. 235)

The students were more likely to disengage from the process of learning when they did not experience a connection to the teacher through a learning relationship.

A culturally responsive teacher is familiar with the beliefs and values held within the cultural communities to which their students belong. A teacher who is culturally responsive believes that how their students are expected to go about learning varies across cultures. Such a teacher gains the necessary cultural knowledge to inform their pedagogical practice and rhetoric so that learners experience learning that aligns with, or at least acknowledges, their cultural identity (Villegas, 1991). A Muslim student should be able to learn as a Muslim, a highlander as a highlander, and an Innuit as an Innuit. One aspect of an effective learning environment is that students feel that their cultural identity is valued.

A culturally responsive learning relationship allows those involved to bring who they are to the learning context. Like the student, the teacher brings a unique combination of knowledge, experiences and values to the learning relationship. Each teacher has evolving knowledge of learning theory, content to teach, pedagogical content knowledge and educational psychology. They also have experience of developing learning relationships, teaching and being a teacher. They are actively learning as connected members of communities of practice, having peers with whom they discuss and align ideas about teaching, learning and being a teacher.

Both the student and the teacher learn through the teacher–student connection. The student will learn subject knowledge and skills through direct instruction, modelling, discussions about learning, questions and feedback on their learning progress. The teacher will learn about what the student knows and understands, and may learn about a different perspective of the subject or topic, or a skill that a student can bring. There is also likely to be non-curriculum or skill based learning that occurs through a student–teacher learning relationship such as developing resilience or understanding different perspectives.

An example of a teacher learning from a student was observed in research into digitally able beginning teachers in their first year of teaching (Starkey, 2010). One of the participating teachers was teaching students about muscle movement and skill development in Volleyball. A student suggested using a digital technology that enabled recording and playback, which could slow down the movement for detailed analysis. The student took the lead to teach the teacher and the class how this could be done. The teacher listened and learnt from the student.

In the digital age valued teachers develop positive learning relationships with their students to establish and maintain an effective learning environment (Figure 4.1). The teacher will be aware of the learner's existing knowledge experiences and cultural background and will consider this when planning pedagogical approaches to use in their teaching practice. Learning occurs as teachers use their knowledge and experiences to listen,

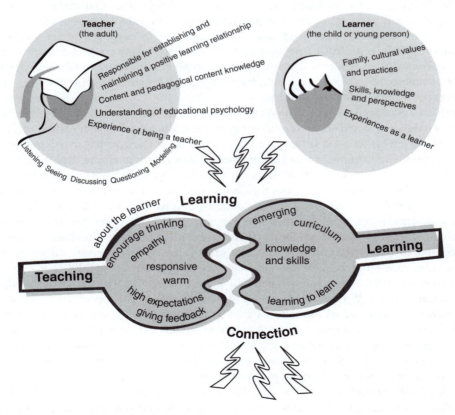

Figure 4.1 Teacher–student learning relationship.

watch, discuss, and question students to encourage thinking, be responsive, and give feedback. It is through this connection between the student and the teacher that learning will occur.

Connections with peers

Connections with peers provide a rich source of learning for students. Schooling structures enable students to establish and maintain connections with peers through which learning can occur. Students are currently allocated age related grade levels and classroom cohorts consist of a group from one or two of these levels. Within the classroom students will establish relationships with peers. In the future structures may differ, but the peer learning relationship is likely to remain. Connectivist learning theory suggests that knowledge develops through relationships and connections. Therefore, being able to establish and maintain learning relationships with peers will be a feature of contributing positively within a digital age society included in school curriculum documentation.

Researchers who have examined student learning within positivist, behaviourist and constructivist frameworks have noted benefits for learning, achievement and classroom environment when collaborative learning occurs within the classroom setting. In John Hatties' 2009 synthesis of meta-analysis peer influences had an effect size of 0.53 which is a strong positive effect on student achievement. Peers influence learning through tutoring, providing friendship, giving feedback and making the class or school a place that students want to come to each day. The social aspects of connections with peers have a strong influence on students. Low classroom peer acceptance has been found to negatively affect academic achievement (Buhs *et al.*, 2001). Being marginalised and not having connections with peers in the classroom limits academic discussion, shared problem solving and collaborative learning that connected peers use. Conversely, friendships provide caring, support and help, and make school an enjoyable place to learn.

From early adolescence social relationships become particularly important and influential. For performance oriented students who compare their achievements with others, this can lead to risk aversion to avoid failure in front of peers. Such students will avoid answering verbal questions and choose an easy option when given a choice to ensure they will be successful. One way of encouraging risk taking in their learning is the use of mastery learning strategies, where the student compares their achievements with set criteria, their own goals or previous performance (attempting more difficult, creative learning tasks). Another is to focus achievement on the group rather than the individual. Both cooperative and competitive teaching strategies have been found to improve student learning. Combining these so that collaborative groups compete against each other can positively motivate student learning provided each group believes they can be successful (Johnson *et al.*, 2000).

Students are social beings and will naturally make connections with each other as they form social groups. Within social groups they will help and support each other in their learning. In a classroom situation a student is more likely to seek assistance from a neighbouring student than the teacher. A common sequence to overcome problems faced during learning that teenage students use when faced with not understanding what to do is outlined in Figure 4.2. This learning behaviour was observed with students who were using online programmes for their learning (Starkey, 2010).

Students will ask each other questions, discuss learning and content, tutor each other, and share metacognitive strategies. Learning through informal peer connections is limited by the combined knowledge, skills and beliefs of the group (which may include

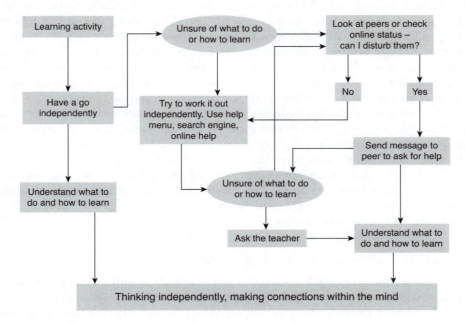

Figure 4.2 Student problem solving during learning – making connections.

misconceptions). Nuthall (2007) suggests that the combined power of peer connections is unleashed when collaboration is deliberate, facilitated and structured with specific social and learning purposes.

Collaborative learning involves learning and evaluating how to learn with others who may not be in the same social group. A teacher in the digital age is able to teach students how to constructively disagree, listen to other people's ideas, suggest and explain their perspectives and understandings, accept and give critique, and tutor their peers. These are all social competencies that can be applied beyond school as students participate in society.

Cooperative learning is a particular approach to learning in which students work in small groups to complete learning tasks to achieve shared goals. David and Roger Johnson are strong proponents of the power of cooperative learning and have carried out research and written extensively in this field. They advocate for cooperative learning to be successful, shared goals and purpose of learning are explicit and each group member has assigned responsibilities and students evaluate not only how well the task was done, but how well each member met their responsibilities within the group. It is a behaviourist teaching strategy which focuses on task completion, therefore is useful for teaching social accountability that can be applied when learning collaboratively. Cooperative learning activities can align with a digital age connectivist perspective when there is a focus on learning rather than solely on task completion. The learning which occurs is through the connections within the group and the task can be open ended allowing opportunities for the group to apply, remix and create knowledge collaboratively.

Developing images of themselves and peers during adolescence and the labelling to signify belonging to certain groups such as 'rebels', 'nerds', or 'sporty' has been found to affect an individual's academic achievement (Berndt, 2004). Students within the labelled group have an image that they wish to portray, which can include attitudes to learning and academic achievement. The image can influence the student's overt attitude to learning and the expectations their peers and teachers have of them. The development of connections across social groups through collaborative learning builds greater cohesiveness within cohorts of peers and can blur the boundary between social identity groups. This does not mean students have to be best friends with those outside their social group. The cultivation of appreciation, understanding and caring across groups can develop or enhance quality collaborative relationships among participants within a learning environment.

Teachers in the digital age encourage and facilitate the connections between peers to enable collaborative learning to occur in their classes. Students learn how to learn through the connections with peers beyond their friendship groups, an important skill set that they should be able to transfer beyond school.

Connections within the learning context

In the digital age the teacher will develop learning relationships with each of the students and students collaboratively learn through peer connections. These two types of connections do not occur independently of each other and a learning group (or class) with their teacher behaves as part of a complex system. If the teacher finds that one student does not understand a particular concept it is likely to influence teaching decisions for the whole group as the teacher may check if others also do not understand. A collaborative group might have developed a short play to illustrate a chemical equation. The sharing of their learning will influence all who observe their actions. The teacher could consider the depth of learning, what to teach the class, individual or group next, and how they could incorporate this type of activity again in the future. The students could learn about the chemical reactions and how chemical equations can be represented through acting.

While schools, education systems, and classrooms can appear to be top-down driven, there is evidence that suggests how the relationships, history and culture within each level influences change from within. The teacher aims to control and develop the learning environment so that students are behaving and learning in the way that they believe to be effective. The students likewise exert control over the environment which influences how they are taught, aligning this with the way that they believe teaching should occur (Wink, 2000). This can lead to conflict. Researchers and teachers have experienced how students meld and shape the way that teachers teach such as the response when a different way of teaching is introduced or a teacher changes from one school to another school with a different culture. For example, when a teacher wanted students to collaboratively learn about their urban environment through inquiry learning then post their findings into Wikipedia, a number of the students did not consider this to be learning that prepared them for exams. It was a different way of learning to what they had experienced previously and in their other classes and therefore they were resistant to this teaching strategy, exerting pressure on the teacher to return to using a more familiar direct instruction approach (Starkey and McCarthy, 2008). The connections and relationships within a classroom influence how teaching and learning occurs. A strong learning relationship can minimise this type of conflict within the learning environment.

The teacher not only connects with individual students, but also with the group they teach as a class. This connection through which learning occurs is strengthened by establishing and maintaining a positive learning relationship. The teacher of the class will acknowledge the differences within the class and also help create a cohesive group identity. A group identity emerges during whole class communications and the sharing of learning or achievements within and beyond the immediate context.

Learning through the teacher–class connection is seen explicitly through direct instruction teaching methods. Direct instruction is a useful teaching strategy to help students learn specific concepts and skills. The teacher tells, shows and models what it is he or she wants the students to learn. The students usually consider the concept or skill in about four different ways through learning activities directed by the teacher. Learning progress is monitored through a variety of formative assessment methods such as questioning, online quizzes or textbook activities and the teacher alters the teaching plan to ensure that students have mastered the particular concept or skill. The learning and feedback process itself further develops the learning relationship the teacher has with the group of students (and individuals).

If students believe that their beliefs, values or efforts are not respected by the teacher, the connection between the teacher and the students will be weakened and this will have a negative impact on the learning environment. Conversely, where the connection is strong and there is respect on both sides the conditions for learning are at their strongest. Clear expectations, how support for learning occurs, each person taking responsibility for their behaviour are all aspects of a learning environment conducive to learning due to effective communication within a learning context.

Through the teacher cohort connection a teacher establishes and maintains an effective learning environment. The teacher can model learning behaviours, such as taking risks in a social context. A teacher who wants to explore different attitudes to drinking alcohol with her class of 14-year-olds could start the lesson by sharing her story about growing up in a different country and the expectations of parents and peers she experienced in the culture. This not only gives a different frame of reference for the students to consider perspectives in their society, but the teacher had modelled taking a risk to share a personal experience which can grow the trust within the learning relationship.

A physical classroom learning environment is determined through the connections within the context. Classroom behaviour management is a term that has its origins within the positivist perspective of knowledge and an authoritarian approach to teaching. While managing student behaviour continues to be a responsibility of teachers, in the digital age the teacher's focus is on creating an effective learning environment where student cohorts are learning how to learn and create knowledge collaboratively as part of a heterogeneous group rather than obedience or compliance. There is a subtle difference with this change in focus (Figure 4.3).

A behaviour management plan that focuses on student learning will aim to maintain and develop effective learning relationships. Such a plan focuses on learning rather than control, rewards and punishments. The principle of 'it is the putting right that counts' from restorative justice practices can be useful when there has been an incident of poor judgement by a student or teacher. This requires the person or group that has had a negative influence on learning to acknowledge what it is that they did and how they will progress positively from there. The latter may be co-constructed with other learners and the teacher. For example, a student may have made the choice to not complete his or her asynchronous collaborative

Situation	Teacher strategies
Focus students to give whole group instructions, feedback or facilitate discussion or sharing of learning.	Use of voice or signal for attention then pause and wait for focus. Body language of expectation – looking at those not focused and when they look at the teacher indicate quietly what you are expecting them to do.
Refocus students on learning when attention has been diverted.	Ask a question directly about the learning. Using the student's name to gain attention with an instruction on how you expect them to behave when focused on learning. 'Tara, the discussion needs focus on atoms.' In a face-to-face situation use of proximity, moving closer to those who are not yet focused.
Refocus students who are disrupting learning of other students.	Give the students a choice – one of the choices is to focus on their learning and let those they are disrupting learn; the other choice ensures that the current disruptive behaviour will end. 'Alex you do not seem to be focused on learning and this is limiting Ishmail's concentration. You can refocus yourself where you are or you can move seats so both you and Ishmail can focus on learning this lesson.' If the student chooses to stay and refocus and this does not work for them then they will be directed to the alternate choice.
Refocus students when they are unresponsive to teacher interventions.	A quiet one-on-one chat with a student that focuses on the student's learning progress and how the teacher cares about the learning progress of the student. Ultimately in the discussion the student will be encouraged to decide what they will do to ensure that their learning will progress and how they can be a positive member of the learning group. This must occur if a student is ever withdrawn from the learning group – the learning relationship with the teacher and peers needs to be rebuilt.

Figure 4.3 Example of a behaviour management plan focused on student learning.

learning task by the deadline and is unable to contribute to the group discussion, which means that the group is missing information to make sense of a concept they are exploring. The learning group could share the consequences of this from their perspective with the student, then discuss as a group how they can change the order of their plans. It would also be useful for group members to share the strategies they use to complete asynchronous tasks to meet deadlines and set a new deadline for the contribution of the student to learning team.

Learning is influenced by the cultural context, in which it occurs. The cultural context is influenced by the teacher and the students who actively participate in the learning process through the relationships they have. The relationships will not just develop by being put within the same context, they require careful nurturing and development by the teacher who has the role of the learning leader.

Connections beyond the classroom

Students can have learning connections beyond the physical classroom environment. These types of connections can be through the World Wide Web. The use of Internet video conversations and online learning environments allow students to establish and maintain learning connections beyond the walls of a classroom. Students may be grouped for formal learning through a course or for a particular learning activity. In 2003–04 I worked with a group of secondary teachers in Connect.ed, an online learning community for 13- to 15-year-olds who were not able to attend school in New Zealand, some of whom were living overseas. The group learnt all their subjects through a co-constructed integrated programme with a mixture of collaborative and independent criteria/goal orientated learning activities. An important aspect of the programme was the development of learning connections between students. As in a classroom context the students naturally interacted socially through the online environment yet needed explicit guidance to scaffold their mastery of collaborative skills and establish relationships through which learning would occur.

Place based learning involves using the local community as a resource for teaching. No matter how many learning connections students have beyond their local area, the community in which they live will remain important as a point of reference. The connections that students have to their local community provide a rich source of learning. Teachers and students can access community resources to develop understanding of a concept, skill or perspective, be the focus of an inquiry, or to actively participate in an activity to enhance the community or environment. Examples of learning activities within the local community are included in Figure 4.4.

Learning connections can be facilitated and developed by teachers when students connect together for study towards scholarship exams, specialist interest studies, or to develop a learning product for a particular purpose. One example is found in language learning, where speakers of one language (for example English) are matched with speakers of the other language (for example Japanese). Through an online learning environment interactions can be facilitated by the two teachers (one in England and one in Japan) where the students teach each other. This could start with a pair of students from each country being matched with a pair from the other class and each producing short video clips to introduce themselves and to pose questions. It could progress to a real time video conversation in

	People	Places
Develop understanding of a concept, skill, or perspective	Interview locals to find different perspectives on waste disposal in the community. Local barista teaches home economics students how to make coffee.	Learning how to measure water flow at a local stream. Study the local landscape to understand how it evolved.
Focus of an inquiry	A notable local person and their contribution to the community. The jobs that people do in the neighbourhood.	Develop solutions to a local town planning issue. Explore the significance of a piece of public art.
Participate to enhance the community or environment	'Adopt a local grandparent' scheme for 6-year-olds. Develop poetry/short film/stage play about the history of the local area and share this within the local community.	Ecological landscape programme at a local site. Lobby local government to gain an improved public outcome (e.g. Better lighting at bus stops).

Figure 4.4 Place based learning – connecting with the local community.

which questions in both languages are alternately asked and answered. The teachers in both countries could align the topics for language development and cultural understanding so that online peer conversations reinforce the learning that is occurring. Tasks could include teaching peers a song in a target language, developing a game show quiz, or producing a short film. Strong professional collaboration and extensive involvement of the teachers is needed to maximise the benefits for the learners.

Another example is students collaborating to develop a response to a challenge set by an external agency. This could be a technological, scientific, artistic or creative challenge such as the development of a web environment or of a prototype solar powered appliance. Students with interest, passion and ability from different learning contexts could collaboratively construct a response to such a challenge under the guidance of one or more tutors (who may be a teacher). This type of learning connection offers an opportunity for the few students across learning environments who share the same interest, talent or passion to extend their learning by connecting and learning with like minded others in a similar way that this occurs through what Chris Anderson called 'the long tail'.

A fourth type of connection that students can make beyond the classroom environment is with experts within the field of learning. A class that is learning about a countries' legal system may have a lawyer share ideas about justice through a visit or videoconference. This may be followed by a week where the students can pose questions through an online forum and receive answers about justice and being a lawyer.

In the digital age students establish connections to learning beyond a physical classroom learning environment. These connections may be face-to-face, virtual or a mixture. Such connections may be with other learners who are in the same learning group or have similar interests to complete a challenge or extend learning. The connections may be to develop place based learning links with the community or to connect with experts in the area of study.

Connections within learning

There is a second type of connection that is important in connectivist learning theory. These are the connections made between ideas, concepts, knowledge or skills. Connections within learning occurs on three levels; the individual learner, the group, and the development of knowledge itself.

The process of perception begins with an object or experience stimulating the body's sensory organs. The sensory organs transform the input energy into neural activity which is transmitted to the brain and processed. Much of what is seen, heard, tasted, and felt is ignored, with the brain deciding which stimulus to analyse and encode.

A constructivist view is that the learner starts from a basis of their prior knowledge, that which is encoded and accessible, then links new experiences to their existing understanding to construct personal understanding. The process of individual learning involves making connections with what has already been experienced or is known by the learner. The learner tries to make efficient use of their brain by connecting new information with what is already understood or known and then develops this further. The brain organises and reorganises itself, creating new memories prompted by experience and learning.

When learning a new concept, such as the agglomeration of business types within the study of geographical spatial variation, the teacher guides students to draw on their existing knowledge, such as local businesses located close to each other. This could be sports shops, the skateboard shops and fast-food outlets. They can then come back to this experience when they consider other types of agglomeration, such as those that occur within manufacturing. The same process occurs when students learn a new skill. If this is a physical skill, such as a chest pass in netball, they will draw on what they know about throwing and catching and draw on their muscle memory to develop skills. Teachers use their knowledge of learning processes and of student interests and experiences to scaffold learning experiences to maximise understanding and mastery of concepts or skills.

Social constructivists have suggested that collaborative learning occurs as connections are made between individual group members' perceptions, ideas, concepts and skills. By connecting the knowledge of the individual members, the combined group develops a shared understanding. Within classroom cohorts peers interact, and in the future whether there are classroom cohorts or more flexible structures, students will learn through connections with their peers with whom they have common background knowledge and those who are different to themselves.

Connectivism recognises that new and novel connections of ideas or concepts can lead to the creation of knowledge. Innovations and new understandings are usually through the connecting together of different ideas, experiences or concepts in different ways. An innovation such as the use of ebooks in society could not have been developed without combining innovations such as digitising text, presenting text on a portable screen, online retail models, and wireless technology. In the digital age connections and innovations which develop knowledge through the combining of ideas could be created by anyone who has access and creative ability. Teenagers currently create mashups where different media are combined together to create something new, sometimes representing a new perspective for the consideration of others.

The process of learning and of knowledge creation involves connecting ideas, concepts, information or data. Individuals make these connections within their brains as they develop their unique perspective and understandings. Groups can combine individual perspectives or understandings to develop shared knowledge. New knowledge can be created through connections made between existing knowledge.

Summary

Complexity theory is a way of considering aspects of the physical and social world which acknowledge that events do not happen in isolation and rarely through a simple cause–effect relationship. In a complex system all the parts are connected. In a digital age schooling system there are three types of connections through which learning or knowledge creation occurs: learning relationships, connections beyond the learning environment and connections between ideas, concepts, information or data.

Learning relationships are the connections between two or more people which focus on learning. In a schooling context the teacher has a leadership role in developing and nurturing these connections which include teacher–student, student–student and class or whole group relationships. It is these relationships with the student through which learning occurs. In addition, digital age students are not restricted to learning within the confines of the four walls of the classroom; they develop learning connections through online or face-to-face discussions with experts and peers beyond the classroom environment.

The process of learning or developing knowledge involves connecting information, data, concepts or ideas. This occurs within the mind of the individual, and between people as a group seeks to gain a shared understanding and can lead to knowledge creation where unique outcomes are developed and shared. Relationships within the classroom and beyond establish the connections through which learning is explored, developed and discussed. The learning needs of the student and teaching decisions a teacher makes will influence the learning that occurs through the connections.

Chapter 5

Creating knowledge

The introduction of digital technologies to society has enabled people to access information, share ideas, and perspectives, and collaborate through a greater number of connections than were previously available. The use of social and professional networks enables the relatively fast development and sharing of ideas, media and information. The ability to create knowledge through these networks is an aspect of participation within a digital age society. Learners in a digital age not only master concepts and skills that enable them to participate in society but they also explore how they can use concepts and skills to create knowledge.

Concepts

A core purpose of compulsory schooling was, and continues to be, to have an educated population that actively contributes to the society in which they live. Society evolves over time, which means that aspects of schooling will also change if it is to continue to meet the aim of school leavers participating in society. In an industrial age students learnt basic skills such as how to read, write and manipulate numbers before leaving school by age 10. As manufacturing and automation increased in society there were fewer labour intensive jobs in both the workplace and the household, therefore a higher level of basic education was needed within the population in order that both genders and all groups of the population could actively and thoughtfully participate. Being educated meant knowing certain concepts and skills as prescribed within national and local curricular. Through the notion of lifelong learning students were taught to be consumers and users of knowledge.

What is important to learn at school evolves as society changes. The focus of learning changed from facts and rules to concepts and skills as the constructivist learning theory became prevalent in the 1900s. A concept is an abstract idea used to make sense of the world in which we live. Subject based learning at school focuses on understanding concepts. Concepts are identified within curriculum documents that students are expected to learn at particular stages of their schooling or over their time within formal education. Examples of concepts are included in Figure 5.1.

Concepts are not tightly bound ideas. They are flexible, with connections within and across subject domains. A three-dimensional ontological architectural framework would be a useful tool for understanding and mapping concepts. Such a framework can underpin curriculum teaching plans and learners' study plans.

The way that a concept is understood, applied, developed and interpreted has cultural nuances. For example, the concept of leadership may vary between a culture where it is

Subject	Example of concepts
Science	Atomic structure, force, circulatory system
Social studies	Leadership, society, democracy
English	Imagery, grammar, poetry
Mathematics	Trigonometry, numbers, fractions
Physical education	Fair play, muscular movement, fitness, coordination
Music	Tone, rhythm, composition

Figure 5.1 Examples of concepts.

believed anyone can put themselves forward to be a leader and the position is decided by popularity, and one in which leaders are chosen by the elders or most educated members of society. The concept of fitness in some cultures will incorporate spiritual along with physical wellbeing; these may be considered separately in other cultures.

Knowledge building

Cognitive processes have been explored from a constructivist perspective and taxonomies that teachers can use as they make decisions about how they teach their students about the concepts have been developed and outlined in curriculum documents. The SOLO taxonomy (Biggs and Collis, 1982) and the modified Bloom's taxonomy (Anderson and Krathwohl, 2000) are frameworks to outline cognitive processes students can use to develop knowledge as they construct understanding and perhaps master concepts and skills. Figure 5.2 aligns the two taxonomies, with a modified Bloom's taxonomy identifying cognitive skills that are deemed by the authors to increase in level of difficulty (although this is debatable and context dependent) and SOLO taxonomy going from the details or aspects of a larger concept or skill through to a holistic understanding able to be applied beyond the context. These taxonomies have been useful in an outcomes based curriculum where the aim of schooling is for students to gain predetermined knowledge and skills.

The first five levels of modified Bloom's taxonomy and the first four levels of the SOLO taxonomy represent knowledge building, where the students are learning a concept or skill. The teacher uses a variety of teaching techniques to guide the students to construct their knowledge of the concepts or skills. Bloom's modified taxonomy has 'create' at the highest level in the cognitive domain and SOLO has extended abstract. Both link the learning with other contexts. At this cognitive level students apply the skill or concept they have been learning to a different context.

Teaching concepts and skills to enable school leavers to actively participate in society requires more than an understanding of cognitive processes. Students need to be taught in ways that motivate and engage them in the learning process so that they develop dispositions and ability to use the knowledge they have built through their schooling. John Dewey (1916) lamented the passive nature of learning that a pupil faced in schools and encouraged the use of interactive learning linked to experiences of the child. It was this

Modified Bloom's taxonomy: cognitive process domain (Anderson & Krathwohl, 2000)	Structure of observed learning outcomes taxonomy (Biggs & Collis, 1982)
1. Remember Recognising, recalling	**Prestructural:** students are simply acquiring bits of unconnected information, which have no organisation and make no sense.
2. Understand Interpreting, exemplifying, classifying, summarising, inferring, comparing, explaining **3. Apply** Executing, implementing	**Unistructural:** simple and obvious connections are made, but their significance is not grasped. **Multistructural:** a number of connections may be made, but the meta-connections between them are missed, as is their significance for the whole.
4. Analyse Differentiating, organising, attributing **5. Evaluate** checking, critiquing	**Relational level:** the student is now able to appreciate the significance of the parts in relation to the whole.
6. Create Generating, planning, producing	**Extended abstract:** the student is making connections not only within the given subject area, but also beyond it, able to generalise and transfer the principles and ideas underlying the specific instance.

Figure 5.2 Taxonomies to build conceptual knowledge or skills.

'liberal' sentiment that saw the emergence of child centred teaching. Dewey also promoted contextual learning, teaching concepts and skills within a context that the student is likely to experience within society rather than learning concepts or skills isolated from the situation in which they can be applied. This idea has come to be known as 'authentic learning'. Discovery and project based learning are teaching strategies that emerged from the desire of having students actively constructing knowledge and using authentic contexts.

Knowledge products

The theoretical basis for child centred learning within teaching programmes is underpinned by Piaget's model of constructivist learning (1952) and later theoretical iterations such as social constructivism. In the 1950s and 1960s learning by discovery or guided discovery based on a scientific research model became a popular option in many primary schools (Shulman and Keislar, 1966). This evolved to become project based learning in the 1990s (also known as inquiry learning). Project based learning typically involved students carrying out an investigation to find an answer to a question which has a positivist basis of finding *the truth*. The methods employed vary between subject contexts (such as a scientific inquiry or hypothesis testing compared to an English research project). A key feature of project based learning is that it usually involves the students developing some type of artefact or 'knowledge product'. A poster, skit, movie, diorama, webpage, podcast, essay and song could all be considered knowledge products when they have been created by students individually or collaboratively to reflect what they have learnt. Seymour Papert introduced the idea of constructionism, where learners learn through constructing a tangible artefact (Papert and Harel, 1991).

While students should be gaining a thorough understanding of the prescribed concepts and skills through project based learning, the reality is that the focus turns to task goals rather than learning goals and the learning becomes incidental to the knowledge product (Bereiter, 2002). This occurs when the teacher focuses on keeping students busy and developing knowledge products as evidence of their students' work.

Meeting diverse learner needs by differentiating instruction can occur by organising different expectations of knowledge products within a classroom situation. Having students learning through project development can free up a teacher to work with groups or individuals within the class to help guide learning at an appropriate level. To achieve this, the tasks must be very clear so that students can individually or in groups continue to work independently of the teacher, thus the focus becomes the task goals rather than learning goals. For example the teacher may guide a student with: 'Once you have found who is the leader you need to find out how they became leader.'

A teacher who wants students to learn about different types of models of national governance can use a project based learning approach. Each student may be allocated a country and guided to research how that country is governed through the following questions: who the leader(s) is/are, how they became leader(s), the process of how laws are decided, who is involved in making decisions about laws, and the subjective well-being or some sort of happiness or contentment scale of the population. The resulting posters would be knowledge products. To develop the posters students have searched for, found and presented information. This does not mean that they have thought about the information that they have included in their presentation. If the activity ends once the posters are complete it would be possible that students have learnt little about models of national governance. The teacher will assess the poster using a rubric (Figure 5.3) and the poster may be photographed and the image added to the student's eportfolio.

The skilful teacher will design activities to guide students through the process of developing their knowledge product while retaining a focus on the learning of concepts and skills. The pedagogical approaches may draw on any or all levels of the modified Bloom's or SOLO taxonomies. The conceptual understanding that was the pedagogical aim will come from these deliberate teaching strategies that focus on students' learning. The teacher in the national governance example will be asking each student questions as they develop their

	Understanding	*Mastery level*
Leadership	Identifies leader and process to gain power	Explains how the leader gained power
Laws	Identifies process used to make laws	Explains how laws are made
Contentment	Identifies the happiness of the nation	Explains how and why the nation has the identified rating for happiness

Figure 5.3 Assessment rubric focused on task goals.

	Understanding	Mastery level
Leadership	Explains how leaders gain power	Able to evaluate connections between different models of governance, law making, and the contentment of the population and draw valid conclusions
Laws	Explains different ways that laws are made	
Contentment	Explains how and why the nations have different levels of contentment	

Figure 5.4 Assessment rubric focused on learning goals.

knowledge product to guide thinking and focus their learning. The posters and individual student knowledge would become a teaching resource to help students explore how each model of governance has strengths and weaknesses which may be culturally and context dependent. This guides students beyond a positivist view of the world towards a critical perspective. The poster will not demonstrate the learning, as the conceptual knowledge for mastery (Figure 5.4) will need to be tested in a different way such as a written test, a conversation or through developing and justifying a plan for a new system of governance for a given context.

Knowledge products can be stored as a record of achievement. Combining the ideas of formative assessment, lifelong learning and project based learning saw the introduction of student portfolios as a method of students demonstrating their learning progress over time. More recently eportfolios have been introduced where students collate examples of their school work and teachers are able to annotate these. There are two components to a portfolio; the process of developing the artefacts that make up the portfolio and the artefacts as a product of student learning. Portfolio use has been associated with increasing the teacher focus on student assessment, learner centred curricular developments and authentic assessment (Wiggins, 1993). These ideas all build on the notion of the teacher's job to help students construct learning and have influenced the perceived importance of having teaching tasks that result in knowledge products which can be added to students' portfolios. Such products commonly reflect task completion rather than mastery learning.

Student motivation is an important aspect of teaching from the child-centred and constructivist learning theoretical perspective. Students who focus on mastery goals, such as mastering conceptual understanding or subject specific skills have been found to spend more time on learning tasks, greater persistence in the face of difficulty and reduced levels of student disruptive behaviour (Kaplan *et al.*, 2010). As a current aim of compulsory schooling is for students to learn particular concepts and skills, it would seem that a mastery focus should underpin pedagogical approaches.

Conceptual artefacts

Bereiter (2002) explored knowledge *building* from a constructivist perspective noting that mastering conceptual knowledge is more than a process and is aimed at creating a product – a conceptual artefact. He defined a conceptual artefact as 'not something in the minds of the students, not something material or visible, but is something students can use' (p. 295). It is the ability to have the knowledge to be able to apply concepts to the world in which they live that prepares them to actively participate in the society in which they live. An example might be learning how business entrepreneurs make a profit. The knowledge may be built by 13-year-old students as they explore a product that they can develop, market and sell, with the profit being donated to a charity as agreed by the class.[1] Students work collaboratively in small groups to explore a product that they believe will be bought at their after school market stall to which family and friends are invited. Students develop a business plan with costings and responsibilities. The groups develop advertisements for their products which are shared prior to the market day.

The market day type learning activity can be a powerful experience if the teacher is able to focus on students *learning* about business entrepreneurship. Each student by the end of the activity should be able to explain factors that make an effective marketing campaign and how a business makes a profit or loss. They will have learnt this during some direct teaching at each stage of the activity and through critical analysis of how their business performed and comparisons with other businesses. It is this learning that is the most important aspect of the activity, not the task itself. The deep understanding of the concept which allows it to be explored, re-examined, and applied to different situations is the conceptual artefact.

The market day learning activity does not include a particular knowledge product but aligns with what John Dewey would consider as authentic learning where students are able to relate their learning to their personal experience, even though the teacher has designed the boundaries of that experience. The task of developing a poster of a country to learn about national governance would not provide students with an authentic learning experience.

A skilled teacher is able to carefully design a project based learning activity with a knowledge product such as a movie, skit or poster and be confident that they will see evidence of students developing conceptual artefacts. For this to happen the teacher's focus needs to be on student learning at all stages of their decision making. The national governance learning activity could develop conceptual artefacts if the students are guided to critically analyse how countries can be governed from a range of perspectives. Such an artefact can be used in the future when considering global events involving national governance.

Conceptual artefacts can be developed through a variety of teaching strategies. Problem based learning is an approach that can include teachers designing whole units around complex, 'ill-structured' problematic scenarios that embody the major concepts to be mastered and understood (Barrell, 2010). Like project learning it is dependent on the skill of the teacher to ensure that the focus of learning remains on the concepts rather than reaching solutions. Problem based learning emerged from the ideas of authentic learning and child centred learning. The British infant school movement, which began in Scotland in 1816, encouraged child centred learning including using 'the child's own question' (Weber, 1971). When using problems to guide student thinking, John Dewey posed the following questions to determine whether a problem is genuine and simulated or a mock problem: Is the problem able to be related to a situation or personal experience? Is it the pupil's own problem, or is it the teacher's or textbook's problem?

The development of a poster, skit, essay, webpage or podcast could require students to apply their understanding of a concept or a skill to a different context, demonstrating an extended abstract learning outcome from the SOLO taxonomy. To do this they would need to draw on their knowledge of what Carl Bereiter describes as a conceptual artefact. A joke can be an example of the use of a conceptual artefact in a connected shared learning environment (Bereiter, 2002). A joke requires a shared understanding of an event or concept. Cartoons are used to explore understanding of historical context and jokes are included in aspects of learning English when embedded in literature, poetry or media. It is unusual to have students using conceptual understanding to produce a comical knowledge product. This is understandable in an outcomes based curriculum as once students have been taught the intended learning outcome then the class moves onto another learning outcome. In the digital age students will continue to gain a deeper understanding of concepts or skills through further exploration of these conceptual artefacts to create knowledge. Jokes could become valid evidence of students exploring the concepts being taught.

Knowledge building to create authentic artefacts focuses on students learning and mastering concepts and skills that have been identified by the curriculum, prescription and/ or the teacher. Thus they are not creating new knowledge, but learning and presenting what is already known and believed to be important for their future participation in society as educated citizens.

There are two ways to consider how school students develop knowledge. The first is within the framework of constructivist learning theory where students learn to be consumers and users of knowledge. The second is underpinned by connectivist learning theory and involves students creating knowledge through connections and critique. Both are important in the digital age.

Knowledge creation

In the digital age access to global and local knowledge has become attainable for people with Internet access. Through the World Wide Web global citizens can join borderless formal and informal learning networks where concepts and ideas to be discussed, debated, developed and shared can lead to knowledge expansion. To be an active participant in such a digital society requires an understanding of how to create and share knowledge through connections. School leavers will need to know how to be critical consumers of knowledge and be able to collaboratively create knowledge to actively participate in a digital age society.

If we are to accept the positivist view of knowledge that the truth can be found through reasoning and scientific testing, then the purpose of schooling could be limited to teaching students how to reason and to learn what is already known. The positivist aims at exploring all avenues until they find the ultimate truth. A complexity theorist considers knowledge to be constantly emerging and existing knowledge can become redundant, re-examined, remixed and reconsidered. Current conceptions of knowledge suggest that there are no limits to knowledge development.

In the digital age a fundamental change in society has been the growth of accessible knowledge:

> Half of what is known today was not known 10 years ago. The amount of knowledge in the world has doubled in the past 10 years and is doubling every 18 months according to the American Society of Training and Documentation (ASTD).
>
> (Gonzalez, 2004, p. 5)

Knowledge can be developed and ideas shared anywhere, anytime through the Internet. People with Internet access can interact online to discuss, comment on what others have said or uploaded, present their own ideas and information, and collaborate through self-selected networks without needing to know computer-based languages. This has led to global connections or networks of like minded individuals who collaboratively or independently develop and link ideas, skills and ultimately share knowledge which is then further developed. Knowledge creation has expanded due to the connection between people and ideas through digital technologies.

The introduction of social networking sites has opened an avenue for the sharing of creative endeavours. This can include blogging, video diaries, uploading videos, photographs, original poetry or music. It can also mean 'mashing' together different resources (music, video, poetry, games) to create a new product that can be uploaded. Websites have been developed specifically to encourage students to share and critique each others' creative endeavours. Scratch is one such example.[2] It was developed by MIT for students to explore programming through developing their own animations using simple programmable blocks. They can download other creations and modify or develop these. What is particularly interesting is that the young people interact with each other, to collaborate, evaluate, and share specialist skills within the environment. One contributor may be particularly interested in developing anime characters which can be used by another who likes to develop games, a third may be interested in adding music to create atmosphere to the games. These structures already exist and are likely to be further developed over time to allow this type of collaboration to occur within the context of learning and creating knowledge that is integrated with the aims of school learning.

If we are to accept the connectivist view of knowledge that it is through connections between parts of a system that knowledge is created, then digital age students will be learning how to participate in a society where all citizens can contribute to the development of knowledge and are not limited to being just consumers of information. While students will continue to need to learn subject based concepts, skills and methodologies, they will also be making the connections between and across subjects and learning to create knowledge in a digital society.

To understand knowledge creation it is useful to examine creativity, which has been described in various ways. Plato compared two types of artists; true artists who bring into birth some new reality, and artists who deal only with appearances and not with reality itself (Plato, 360 BCE, as cited in Anderson, 1959, p. 57). He was making a distinction between artists who were skilled at manipulating tools to reproduce what is already known and artists who were able to show something new as a result of manipulating the tools. The former could be seen as developing an individual's knowledge by reproducing what is already known, the latter is being creative, developing new knowledge. Taking this definition, being able to reproduce an existing reality through a knowledge product would be skilful rather than a demonstration of creativity in the sense of creating new knowledge.

The development of a poster, skit, essay, webpage or podcast to demonstrate students' understanding of concepts or skills as taught by the teacher and as mandated by curriculum or prescriptions is the equivalent of an artist reproducing what is already known. Assuming that the students do not just copy the information and the design of the teaching activity requires the students to have developed the conceptual understanding or skills, then students would be building knowledge as they learn the prescribed concepts or skills.

A second definition of creativity comes from an educational setting. The National Advisory Committee on Creative and Cultural Education in England gives a schooling based definition of creativity as: 'Imaginative activity fashioned so as to produce outcomes that are both original and of value' (NACCCE, 1999, p. 29). This aligns with Plato's definition, but with the added idea that the product must have value. In the case of creating knowledge this could be interpreted as being of value to at least one other person.

Knowledge creation occurs when students develop ideas from concepts and skills and share this beyond the classroom environment to gain critical feedback. Connectivist learning theory suggests that knowledge creation occurs through connections; from connecting together ideas, through collaboration, or the mashing of different media, concepts or skills. Knowledge creation could include exploring something that is 'known' from a different perspective, mashing concepts or skills, a reinterpretation of an idea, or the results of research.

Student can develop ideas that produce outcomes that are both original and of value within schooling contexts. An example of knowledge creation was explained by a colleague who teaches home economics. Her 16-year-old students in home economics examined the impact of globalisation on food. The government at the time was considering food labelling legislation. This provided an opportunity for the students to make a submission to a Select Committee, a group of politicians who were considering legislation on the topic. The class carried out research using literature, reports and their own research to develop an informed perspective on the issue that they could submit. This type of activity involves students creating knowledge. The students had to learn about the concept of globalisation as applied to food and nutrition. They considered what food labelling requirements should be mandated and the implications of what they were recommending. The knowledge they created may have been from a different perspective to the existing literature and knowledge on the topic due to the context and age of these knowledge creators. This type of knowledge creation is powerful learning when the aims of schooling are considered. If an aim is for students to become active participants in society then having students experiencing the process of making an informed submission to influence the laws of the country is a significant example of participatory action. Prior to the digital age, such a learning activity would have taken a long time to organise and complete. Gaining access to credible sources on the topic and being able to discuss with experts in the field would have been difficult to achieve and a written and posted submission process may have further restricted times. Online access to the literature and information networks on the topic, and the online submission process, made this a feasible learning activity that would not have been possible prior to the digital age.

Knowledge is rarely developed in isolation, and between the students' initial ideas and the creative product, there will be critique and evaluation. The phenomenon of the long tail (Anderson, 2006) means that through social or professional networks, learners who may be creators of knowledge are able to connect with others in the world with similar interests. Collaboration and connections through digital technologies allow sharing and critique of knowledge as it develops. This feedback can be used to ascertain whether the created knowledge has value. Sharing and critiquing of evolving knowledge could be an important aspect of learning and participating in a digital age society.

In the study of national governance the students may have mastered the ideas of how different countries are governed and why there are different models. They may then use these conceptual artefacts to explore how countries might be governed in the future, mashing together ideas such as one set of values and beliefs with another type of governing structure. This could be trialled and shared within an online virtual environment and critiqued by participants. There would be potential for the findings to be shared.

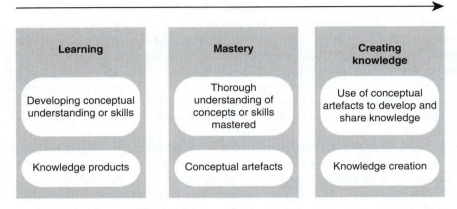

Figure 5.5 Learning, mastery and knowledge creation.

The difference between learning, knowledge products, conceptual artefacts and knowledge creation are outlined in Figure 5.5. Learning involves the process of developing conceptual understanding or skills. Mastery is when the concepts or skills have been learnt thoroughly, not at 50 per cent level, and can be demonstrated through conceptual artefacts. Knowledge creation occurs when concepts and/or skills are examined through a different perspective or combined to consider a new idea or solution. All are valid teaching aims within school learning in the digital age when used thoughtfully through the process of pedagogical reasoning.

The schooling sector in most countries have moved from tests that almost exclusively emphasise mastery of facts and rules, to students demonstrating they understand concepts and have mastered skills which in turn drive curricula with the same emphasis. Through the creation of knowledge conceptual understanding is tested and expanded.

Learning in the digital age from a student's perspective will include a number of aspects (Figure 5.6). Students will have a range of learning tasks that will help them to build conceptual understanding with an aim to developing mastery level understanding. This is not new and has been the focus within school based education since constructivist learning became the dominant influence within teacher education. What is new is that this is not the ultimate goal of schooling; students will not only achieve mastery, but will be expected to explore the concepts and skills further through critique and creativity as they connect with other ideas and ultimately share their ideas beyond the learning environment.

Students learn concepts or skills that the teacher or the curriculum has identified as appropriate for the time and context. These are explored through learning activities which employ a range of cognitive processes while focusing on learning about the concept or skill. These may incorporate aspects from all levels of Bloom's modified cognitive taxonomy. The learning activity that focused on mastering the concept of national governance diversity could include analysis of one form of governance, understanding leadership, evaluating data, and creation of a poster.

The learning activities may be discrete activities that directly link to the concept or skill with the connecting ideas shared after activities are completed, or each activity may build on

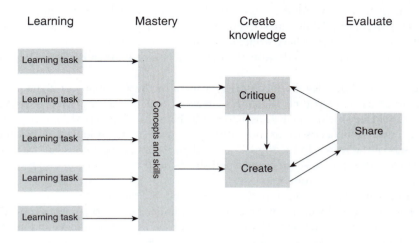

Figure 5.6 Learning in the digital age.

the learning of the previous one following a structure such as the SOLO taxonomy. The market day learning activity which was focused on students learning the concept of entrepreneurship involved the students learning about marketing, advertising, profit and product development before being applied to their market day context. The learners examined aspects of the concept before considering the concept holistically. Learning the concept of chemical equations will be a more linear process, with students being scaffolded through stages of understanding molecular structures and balancing chemical equations before grasping the concept and skill.

Mastery of a concept or skill is when the learner has a thorough understanding, they can discuss, explain and demonstrate mastery within the learning context and consider applications beyond the context. To be successful the student must be making connections between the learning tasks and the concepts or skills that they are to master. The students may be fully engaged in a learning task and meet all the set requirements but without explicit connections between the set 'work' and the concepts or skills students will focus on task goals, and learning, if it occurs, is incidental. This would be the case in the national governance activity. Students could focus on each task that they were asked to complete and produce a poster that had the information about the leader, how laws are made and the general satisfaction of the population, but without considering this information within the context of the concepts most students would not learn more than a few facts.

Once students are confident with their understanding of the identified skills and concepts they are then able to consider how they can be applied to other contexts, how they fit with other concepts or skills and explore the boundaries of each concept or skill. This level of thinking can result in knowledge being created. Students need to think critically as they apply creativity to explore concepts or skills in depth. For example, the students studying national governance may have completed the learning tasks and understood that there are different models of leading and ruling a nation, and that each model has strengths and weaknesses. They could then explore this further to consider what models might be best for a cultural context that they are familiar with. This would require them to create a number of scenarios and critically evaluate each using the conceptual knowledge they have developed studying a number of different systems. From this they could create an idealised system of governance that they believe would have a high satisfaction rating for their chosen context, they could evaluate this and justify their choice. This could then be shared beyond the classroom context.

Sharing ideas beyond the classroom context is enabled by the availability of digital technologies. As students develop their thinking to beyond that of learning what is already known, they should be sharing their insights beyond the walls of the classroom. A poster can be put on a wall within a classroom and probably not examined, but looked at, by other students or users of the room. In the digital age students should expect constructive feedback on their ideas through what they create and share and the responses should be from beyond the physical classroom context.

An example of creating knowledge is outlined in Figure 5.7. Students of home economics in the digital and globalised world may be expected to understand two complex concepts – multinational food production and ethical food choices. To gain this understanding the teacher may set a range of tasks, explicitly connecting the learning with the students' developing conceptual understanding. The first task could involve students working in pairs to design a meal that they believe is a healthy choice if they were cooking a meal for a group of friends. Under the menu the students list all ingredients including cooking substances, garnishes and dressings. At the conclusion of this activity the teacher guides a conversation about the origins of food, possible travel distances and what was known about the farming and agricultural practices of the farmers where the food has come from. The second task would be for the students to investigate their listed ingredients to find out where they originate. This could include contacting manufacturers and supermarkets if the food labelling is unclear. The information gathered can be presented on a map or interactive web page, and analysed through an online carbon footprint calculator. The ethical implication of the travel distance of the food is then discussed to focus learning on

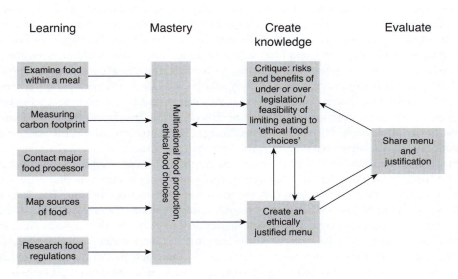

Figure 5.7 Home economics learning in the digital age.

the conceptual understanding. The third activity would be to explore the farming and agricultural practices, and food safety legislation, of the countries that the ingredients originate from and compare these to the home nation. The students may identify or be encouraged to explore ethical considerations and food safety concerns which could exist in their own or other nations, which would imply that a multinational food supply could be beneficial or problematic for the consumer of the food.

To demonstrate mastery of the concepts students explain how the meal they designed represents the concept of multinational food production and the ethical implications of knowing or not knowing the origin of the ingredients for the meal.

Students could then explore how they could develop a statement about ethical choices for a sustainable and healthy future. This statement would need to critically analysed and considered before students develop a menu that replaces or modifies the menu from the first task to demonstrate how they could make what they believe are ethical choices. The class group could explore and develop a joint statement about multinational food supply and ethical choices of food which could be integrated into the school's 'food for thought' website, which is globally accessible. The menus could be shared online and feedback sought from the online food community. If students had focused on sourcing locally produced ingredients there could be the opportunity to share the menus at local food suppliers such as farmer markets, butchers or greengrocers with a link to an online site for feedback. The feedback received would inform iterations of their menus and understanding of the concepts.

Through this process of creating knowledge using the concepts of multinational food production and ethical food choices the students will revisit their understanding of the concepts and question the boundaries of the concepts. For example, they may find that there is a smaller carbon footprint in producing a particular food crop in country X and importing it to country Y, than producing it locally in country Y, due to the climatic and soil conditions.

Connections would be made through linking ideas and connecting with people. Students would learn through conversations with their in class peers, their teacher, and external experts such as the growers or manufacturers of food products. Ideas would be developed through connecting local and international consumer information and regulations with conceptual understanding of multinational food supply and ethical food choices. Using the local and personal context as a starting and final point in the learning assists the students to make connections to their experiences and how these concepts are relevant to their lives.

The connection between concepts and skills within and across subjects contributes to the expansion of knowledge through applying concepts and skills from one context or subject domain to another. Further learning and knowledge can be created through integrating different subject domains with home economics. A student studying economics could explore the economic impact of legislation around food miles on the producing and consuming countries. A student of art, music or drama could create a strong message using their conceptual understanding of ethical food choices that could be shared online. A student of social studies could explore how tight regulations or lack of regulations can impact on the food choices that are made in society. Students of English could explore the language of the various groups with vested interests. A student of geography could explore the different cultural perspectives that are present in multinational food production. This example of learning illustrates how students in the digital age will learn to create knowledge and have that knowledge critiqued beyond the classroom learning environment.

Summary

In a digital world, active citizens in society are not only users and consumers of knowledge, but also creators and critics of knowledge. School learning in the digital age will be focused on mastering concepts and skills that students will need to participate in their society. It will also include learning how to use the concepts and skills they have mastered to create knowledge, with the resulting ideas being shared and evaluated beyond the immediate learning context.

Chapter 6

Critical thinking

> It is the mark of an educated mind to be able to entertain a thought without accepting it.
>
> Aristotle (384–322 BCE)

In the digital age an extensive range of information and data are available within seconds through mobile digital devices. Information can be developed and shared by anyone with Internet access. Thus, to actively participate in a digital age society students will need to learn to think critically about the information they are accessing or sharing, their own learning processes, the feedback they receive and their academic progress.

Critical thinking

Critical thinking has long been considered an important skill to integrate into school based learning. Being able to analyse, critique, judge, compare and contrast, evaluate, assess, reason and test hypotheses are a few of the skills often listed as central to being able to think critically (Ennis, 1987; Halpern, 1998; Sternberg, 2003). Across most dictionaries, the terms analysis, evaluation and judgement are used to define critique or critical thinking. The Oxford Online dictionary defines critique as *to evaluate in a detailed and analytical way*. A definition for school based critical thinking in the digital age could include *analytical evaluation through the deliberate and thoughtful application of metacognitive strategies*.

Critical thinking in education could be used by a 15-year-old to develop a schema to evaluate what makes certain musicians popular, or by a 5-year-old to consider whether two objects are the same weight, providing they used careful analysis and did not just guess the answer. How critical thinking has been incorporated into teaching and learning processes has varied and has been influenced by the beliefs and values of the time and the theory of learning underpinning teaching practice.

A positivist perspective of knowledge, teaching and learning would consider critical thinking within the framework of learning what is factual or correct. In 1962 Ennis, who was a prominent writer in the field, construed critical thinking as the *correct assessment of statements*. The dominant use of critical thinking within a positivist learning environment would be to evaluate whether something was the truth. Scientific inquiry using hypothesis testing is an example of the use of critical thinking within positivist school based learning. This type of critical thinking continues to be useful in the digital age, although it now involves analysing an idea or hypothesis through observation, reasoning or deduction to evaluate how likely it is to be correct rather than reaching a predestined conclusion or truth.

As post-structural ideologies infiltrated education and constructivist perspectives of learning became widespread, a gradual change of pedagogical processes occurred which is reflected in how critical thinking was integrated. For example, Ennis in 1987 (25 years after his former definition) suggested that critical thinking was *reasonable reflective thinking focused on deciding what to believe or do*. A constructivist considers critical thinking within the framework of developing a learner's understanding or skills by connecting what they are experiencing with what they already know. The rise of inquiry or project based learning where generic critical thinking skills were taught and applied is an example of one way critical thinking has been incorporated within a constructivist learning environment.

Inquiry or project based learning within social sciences has tended to utilise formulaic, transferable structures underpinned by ideas from information literacy. This could involve identifying a problem or issue, researching to find a range of solutions, evaluating the different solutions and justifying what the best outcome would be, for example Eisenberg *et al.*'s (1999) 'Big6' and Gwen Gawith's Action Learning (1988). An underpinning idea of this approach is to link students' school based learning with the kind of messy problems that they will encounter in their everyday lives; problems that may not have a straightforward correct answer, but which will require thoughtful consideration before coming to a decision. There may not be one right answer, which indicates a different view of knowledge than seen in a positivist paradigm. Within project based learning critical thinking may occur across an inquiry and would usually be present in the final stages of evaluating and making a judgement.

In 1987 Peter Facione brought together a group of 46 experts to develop a consensus about the meaning of critical thinking within the context of school based education and published the resulting definition and key points of the discussion in 'The Delphi Report' (Facione, 1990). The group worked from the assumption of the time that critical thinking was essentially a tool of inquiry. The experts defined critical thinking as 'purposeful, self-regulatory judgement which results in interpretation, analysis, evaluation, and inference, as well as contextual considerations upon which that judgement is based' (p. 3). This definition is applicable to teaching and learning in the digital age as it can be applied to the process of knowledge creation.

The Delphi Report group identified 15 dispositions, including being habitually:

> inquisitive, well-informed, trustful of reason, open-minded, flexible, fair-minded in evaluation, honest in facing personal biases, prudent in making judgements, willing to reconsider, clear about issues, orderly in complex matters, diligent in seeking relevant information, reasonable in the selection of criteria, focused on inquiry, and persistent in seeking results which are as precise as the subject and the circumstances of inquiry permit.
>
> (Facione, 1990, p. 3)

These critical thinking dispositions appear to be underpinned by a positivist epistemology where the truth is being sought. Dispositions for the digital age include exploring differing perspectives and may aim for questions or new ideas rather than results. Such dispositions could be learnt through school based programmes, which include the teaching of critical thinking.

Whether critical thinking should be taught as a generic skill, able to be transferred across different learning contexts as in project based learning, or taught within specific subjects has been considered and debated by education researchers and curriculum designers such as Ennis (1989). From a complexity theory perspective it would seem that both are important. Students learn to think critically about the nature and the epistemological basis of the subject to enable them to understand what they are learning and how this connects to the collective knowledge of the subject. The understanding and knowledge of subject specific concepts and methodologies will underpin student learning as they create, share and critique knowledge. Therefore critical thinking skills should be learnt within the context of a specific subject domain then explored within other contexts. A learning programme would enable students to transfer the application of critical thinking skills through explicit links and comparisons across subject domains. Explicitly considering critical thinking skills within and across subjects aligns with connectivist learning theory.

Critical thinking about information, data and resources

The use of critical thinking has been identified as particularly important in the digital age as relatively quick access to a wide range of information means that the user needs the ability to critically evaluate the validity and relative value of information accessed. In the past the library, a book, or an expert (e.g., a teacher) were the student's source of knowledge, and the value or validity was unlikely to be questioned (Rowlands *et al.*, 2008). When the Internet was originally introduced to school based learning programmes a number of educators were reluctant to use it as a teaching resource as the information may not contain correct facts. This view reflected the limited information available at the time through the Internet, the lack of social media where large numbers of people and experts were developing knowledge, and a positivist orientation to schooling (purpose is to learn truths). The abundance of information at the touch of a digital technology means that learners need to be able to critically evaluate its relevance, validity and significance. This type of critical thinking expands the scientific orientation of critical thinking using reasoning to evaluate credibility.

Over the years a learner's analysis of sources becomes more sophisticated and complex. A 5-year-old might use critical thinking when deciding whether information is true, false or could be true, when compared with their current understanding (for example, 2 + 2 = 5; a blue polar bear). A 15-year-old would examine information using multiple methods of analysis to consider the relevance, validity and significance.

To ascertain the relevance of a source or data the learner needs to understand the purpose and have criteria which they can use to make a judgement. The clearer they are about the purpose the easier it is to judge whether something is relevant. To evaluate validity may involve examining the source, the expertise of the author, when something was written, or comparing the information with what else is written. The significance of information or data can be ascertained by considering the validity, relevance and the information within the context of other available information.

The way that the significance, validity and relevance of information are ascertained varies across subject domains. In social sciences the credibility of the source can be important. In science the scientific method used to reach a conclusion can be critical to the validity. In the digital age learners will develop critical thinking skills that can be used generically and critique specific to the subjects they study.

Critical thinking while learning concepts and skills

The rise of social networking and the ability to collaborate online enables learning through connections and relationships which may be at a distance. Learning through an online environment can occur asynchronously where individuals collaboratively develop a shared understanding of a concept or construct some type of representation of their combined knowledge.

An example of critical thinking while learning concepts and skills might be a group of students from three schools problem solving an environmental issue. The process they follow would be grounded in the epistemologies of science and social sciences. They would be supported and guided by a teacher and may seek advice from an external expert such as a trained and practising environmentalist as they explore the issue from their own contexts. This would involve critical thinking – careful analysis which includes evaluating and judging the extent of the issue or problem. They could then explore solutions to the problem that would work for their contexts. This would involve researching a range of aspects which will need to be connected by the group. There may be legislative aspects, scientific solutions and/or technological innovations. Through discussion which could be in a shared space on the Internet such as a virtual learning environment, videoconferencing or messaging, the various options identified could be analysed and evaluated collaboratively. The public acceptability for possible solutions may be explored and once the group and their expert have thoroughly critiqued their methodology, findings and feasibility of their solution they could share their findings with the school board, local council, Minister for the Environment or relevant official or expert who is in a position to consider the students' findings. Or they could post their findings on a social networking site through which they gain critique and feedback which will inform changes to their solutions, and which may also raise awareness and support to implement change.

Collaborating to examine an environmental issue involves critical thinking, making connections and participating in society which aligns with the purpose of compulsory national schooling. The teacher guides the students through the process to help them develop critical thinking skills and make the connection with an expert for the peer critique. The exact nature of the learning and the outcome will not be known, which can be uncomfortable for a teacher who is most familiar with teaching in an outcomes based or prescriptive curriculum.

Each subject area has critical thinking skills specific to the way that information or knowledge is explored and developed within that domain. The following examples briefly outline critical thinking within history, physical education, science, health and English curriculum studies.

Students of history analyse the past, taking into consideration the differing perspectives in the past and among those who have since interpreted society or events. This is known as historical thinking and involves critical analysis; evaluating evidence and making judgements. Historical thinking is a process that does not necessarily end in a definitive answer, rather a current interpretation.

Physical education requires students to critically analyse body movement, aligning physiological theory with the practice of movement for a purpose. Digital technologies can be used in the analysis by tracking movement, which allows detailed measurement of speed, angle, direction, and style to be compared to models of movement. The learner is able to critique the physical movement drawing on physiological theory.

There are a number of ways that students think critically within biological sciences. Students may be learning about evolutionary adaptations by examining quadruped movement, comparing the speed, agility and strength of a range of species with their habitat and dietary requirements. The students may learn in pairs, examining online video clips of animal movement, comparing and contrasting the links between the animal physiology and their lifestyle and deduce some conclusions and questions. The pairs will be using critical thinking to explore the different links and explanations they identify. The pairs could share their findings and questions in the online learning environment with other groups in the class, and possibly beyond the class, then develop a hypothesis to test. Testing a hypothesis in science is another subject specific critical thinking methodology.

Twelve-year-old students studying health and English think critically as they explore persuasive media images. Students examine a range of advertisements across media sources or within one particular media. They consider how the advertisements capture audience attention and what messages are given. They then choose a product that could have harmful effects on health and redesign an advert for the product which uses similar imagery, sound and visual techniques but highlights the negative effects of using the product. They create a 'badvert' which is uploaded to a wiki (a badvert is an advertisement which highlights the negative aspects of a product rather than the positive). The wiki can be a source for peer review and exemplars for students of future years. Critical thinking occurs as they evaluate and judge commercial advertisements and as they develop their own badverts.

Learning in the digital age includes thinking critically, in a detailed and analytical way, about the nature of the subject being studied, concepts, and methodologies within the subject. Conceptual understanding will be developed through individuals thinking critically, peer and structured group critique.

Critical thinking about learning progress

In the digital age a learner is taught to critique their own learning progress. If the purpose of schooling is to prepare the future population to participate in society then they need to develop the skills and capacity to learn beyond formal education. Learning to learn occurs through the processes of planning, critique and reflection.

Metacognition is the process of thinking about thinking. Students learn how to plan, monitor and regulate their cognitive processes while developing conceptual understanding and skills. Metacognitive processes are strategies for learning, acquiring resources and skill development. Thinking aloud, where students talk through the processes that they are applying, can help peers to understand the metacognitive strategies being used. Tools may also be learnt, such as Edward De Bono's thinking hats, that can then be applied to examine a social issue.

Metacognitive strategies can be subject specific. To successfully solve mathematical problems students need to be able to draw on number strategies to guide their thinking. A useful metacognitive strategy is to check an answer by using an alternative mathematical process or the same one used but in reverse. This process requires analysis and judgement.

In history the ability to write an effective essay requires students to learn how to structure and develop a paragraph before moving into the structure of an essay. Students may learn to structure a paragraph in a history essay with a statement, explanation, examples and summary or link to the next paragraph. The history teacher typically scaffolds learners to be able to structure their writing by carefully analysing paragraphs to identify the structural features, then to write paragraphs with an awareness of the structure they are using. Feedback on paragraph structure by peers and the teacher will help develop confidence and familiarity with this metacognitive strategy. The student may practice this metacognitive process until it becomes an automatic part of their writing process.

Generic metacognitive strategies can be transferred across subjects. Understanding brain function can help students to monitor and plan their cognitive processes. When they need to memorise an aspect of their learning they can use techniques that efficiently place information into their long-term memory. For example, if they are developing a speech which must be presented without notes students might develop cue cards, then visualise each card using repetition at set times through a day and over a week, checking accuracy each time. This technique can be transferred to a science context as students learn about the elements within the periodic table. This requires memorisation so generic visual memory and use of flash cards or mnemonics can help. The metacognitive strategies increase in effectiveness when they are explicitly analysed by the user or the group and the transfer across subjects or contexts is considered.

If students in the digital age are expected to create and share knowledge they will need to learn how to plan, monitor and regulate their cognitive processes. Teachers need to scaffold students as they learn metacognitive skills; this could include initially using templates and questions, or using checklists at set times in the learning process. The teacher slowly takes the scaffolding away as students begin to use metacognitive skills independently and develop the conditional knowledge of when and why to apply various cognitive skills.

Generic questions to monitor learning progress might include:

- What am I aiming to learn?
- What resources, knowledge and skills do I need to learn this and how can I access these?
- How long do I have? How long for each process?
- Who can give me feedback on my learning? When?
- How will I know that I have successfully learnt this?

Students who are learning about advertising and healthy or socially responsible choices may be developing *badverts*. The context of learning: students have studied advertising campaigns and the techniques that advertisers can use to persuade consumers to buy their products. The teaching aim is for the students to learn to be discerning consumers, critical of the ubiquitous advertising that is present in many facets of their lives. They have examined badverts developed by students in previous years and developed an evaluation rubric to guide their own learning. Figure 6.1 is an example of a rubric students may develop that they can use to think critically about their own and their peers' badverts.

Being aware of the teacher's learning intentions has emerged within a constructivist learning approach and aligns with outcomes based curriculum. Understanding the intent of the learning tasks that a teacher has set can be motivating for some students as they feel involved rather than feeling that the learning is just a chore they have to do on their journey through school. Evelyn Ng (Ng and Bereiter, 1991) identified three different goal orientations that students have in school based learning. The first is task completion goals, where the student aims to complete the tasks set by the teacher. This is a behaviourist orientation that can be encouraged when the teacher has a greater focus on teaching than on learning. These students are motivated by the approval they receive when they complete the tasks; they may learn what the teacher intended as they complete the tasks. Their self-analysis of

BADVERTS	Progressing	Achieved	Mastered
Message content	Message tells you why the product is not good for your health or is socially irresponsible.	Message gives clear reasons why the product is not good for your health or socially irresponsible.	The clear message is likely to cause people to consider the health or social consequences of using the product.
Message delivery	Message has some similar aspects to the original.	Message is clear and has similarities to the original advertisement.	The different aspects of the badvert mirrors the original advertisement.

Figure 6.1 Badverts' evaluation rubric.

progress is unlikely to involve careful critical evaluation of their progress towards their goals. These students respond well to checklists and a teacher can build critical thinking into listed tasks. For example:

- Discuss the project with my study buddy (ideas, the plan, and resources).
- Identify an advertised product which can be unhealthy or socially irresponsible.
- Explore how it is unhealthy or socially irresponsible and list the sources used.
- Evaluate sources and content of information.
- Health teacher gave critique and altered my notes for unhealthy or socially irresponsible effects of the product.
- Analysed an advert using method learnt in English.
- Peer gave critique on the critical analysis of an advert.
- I critiqued a peer's analysis using method learnt in English.
- Include peer critique in summary of analysis.
- Received English teacher critique and altered summary of analysis.
- Planned a badvert using analysis and ideas about unhealthy aspects of product.
- Identified skills needed to develop badvert.
- Self-evaluated the developing badvert using evaluation rubric.
- Posted badvert into virtual learning environment.
- Read critique of my badvert.
- Altered badvert after reading critique in the virtual learning environment.
- Discuss and evaluate my badvert and the process with my teacher.

The second orientation is when the student is focused on learning goals. This orientation is underpinned by mastery learning where the student aims to learn skills or concepts and compares his or her progress towards mastering these. The student will critically analyse their progress using criteria from the teacher or that has been co-constructed. They are intrinsically motivated through the self-satisfaction they gain from their learning progress and frustrated when unable to progress or access support. An assessment rubric such as Figure 6.1 can help the student who is focused on learning goals.

The third orientation identified by Ng and Bereiter (1991) is knowledge building goals. These students make links (or connections) between their learning in class and ideas beyond the immediate learning environment. These learners actively consider the ideas and concepts as they are learning, which may or may not include critical analysis.

Their self-critique will involve evaluating their learning progress through the innovation and links they have made. These students respond well to learning activities that include knowledge creation.

There is no evidence that the three orientations are mutually exclusive, that students are in one orientation for all facets of their learning or that students are unable to be reorientated.

Once templates and task lists are introduced there is a danger that the focus moves from the learning to task completion. The digital age teacher ensures that the focus does not move from the thinking to racing through the tasks by focusing communications on the learning that is occurring. For example, instead of asking students if they have had their work peer critiqued, the teacher asks, 'How did the critique your peer gave you influence your thinking about the product you are studying?' Or, 'How do you know that this is an outcome of using this product?' Critique is focused on learning; the process and the outcomes of the thinking process.

A teacher may introduce a scaffold system to guide student learning that is less step-by-step, such as the example in Figure 6.2. In this example the students self-regulate their

Plan for self regulated learning	My learning buddy: James		
What I aim to learn:	How advertisers persuade people to buy a product. How some advertised products are unhealthy or socially irresponsible.		
Focus of learning	Thinking strategies	Resources	When and Where
How are certain advertised products unhealthy or socially irresponsible?	Research and summarise why a product from an advertising campaign can be unhealthy. Get critical feedback from the health teacher.	Advertisements. Internet resources. Health teacher.	
What techniques do advertisers use to persuade users to buy products?	Analyse how the advertisement is designed to attract attention and give its message. Get critical feedback.	List developed in class. Peer then English teacher to critique.	
Create a 'badvert'	Compare progress against evaluation rubric. Identify skills needed to develop the advert (image altering, film making, voice recording).	Assessment rubric. Digital/artistic materials. Peer or mentor with expertise to help teach skills needed.	
How effective is my badvert?	Listen and consider critique, modify badvert and repost within the virtual learning environment.	Place to share and receive peer critique.	

Figure 6.2 Plan for self regulated learning.

learning using the plan as a guide. The plan serves as the focus of teacher–student interactions about learning progress.

The development of learning plans can be teacher directed, co-constructed or student directed. The purpose of a plan is to guide critically and monitor student progress in learning, avoiding focusing on task completion. Giving peer feedback is a skill that students can learn in conjunction with receiving feedback and self-evaluation of learning progress. The giving and receiving of critique is an important aspect of knowledge creation.

Critical thinking and creating knowledge

Students think critically as they explore the boundaries and integrate concepts and skills to create knowledge. Comparing what is known with alternative realities, perspectives, explanations, or possibilities requires critical thinking such as comparing, contrasting, analysing, evaluating and synthesising.

The exploration and development of badverts includes students critiquing an advertised product to evaluate the benefits and problems associated with its use. With teacher guidance, this analysis involves critical thinking as students judge the credibility of claims of harmful or beneficial effects and explore possible negative effects of a product or how it may be perceived if viewed through a different cultural lens. Students create knowledge as they integrate the concepts of advertising and critical consumption with media presentation skills to develop the badvert. In doing so they think critically about their progress and their emerging ideas.

Emerging ideas are shared and critiqued for assessment and validation. Sharing occurs through connections with peers, the teacher, and beyond the immediate learning environment. This is not a one-way process in that the students receive feedback as part of a discussion with the opportunity to think critically about the critique and to modify their ideas or product as a result. Critical thinking is an important aspect of learning, underpinned by the belief that knowledge is debatable. Receiving and giving of critique is an aspect of knowledge development through connections.

Critical thinking and assessment

Giving feedback to students about their learning is at the core of effective teaching practice. Paul Black and Dylan Wiliam (1998) examined the research on assessment within schools and identified effective feedback as an important component that assists student learning. While the authors were considering assessment from a teacher assessing student perspective, in a digital age learning context feedback is not limited to that given by a teacher. It can be reflective, with the learner critiquing their own progress against criteria; it can be peer feedback; or it can be feedback from an external expert or interested person.

Effective feedback for a learner has a number of components. The word 'assess' comes from the Latin verb 'assidere', meaning 'to sit with'. This implies it is something that is done 'with' learners and not 'to' students (Green, 1999). An exchange such as a discussion between the learner and the assessor can clarify misconceptions, misunderstandings or difficulties that the student might be having in understanding what the assessor is suggesting. Such an exchange will enhance the understanding of the assessor of the ideas or thinking of the student and thus be an opportunity for both to think critically about concepts, skills and the learning process.

Learners need to think critically about the feedback they receive if it is to inform their learning. A student who receives an assessment grade without having a discussion with their teacher or the opportunity for further learning on the topic or skill is unlikely to consider why they received that grade, what they had learnt, which concepts or skills they had not mastered and what learning they will undertake to improve the grade or their knowledge of the subject. Ruth Butler (1999) examined 132 students aged 11 and 12 as they responded to assessment feedback they received. She found that students given only marks made no gain from the first to the second assessment. Students given only comments scored on average 30 per cent higher. Effective assessment that informs student learning occurs during the learning process and encourages students to think critically about their learning progress.

The students learning about the messages given by the media have developed their badverts. Consider three types of critique within this learning scenario.

The students present their badverts to the class and the teacher looks at the product and listens to what the students have to say then gives the learners critique in written or verbal form (Figure 6.3). The critique is based on the criteria developed in class using terminology developed in the learning process. The student may learn something from the critique given if they have the opportunity to apply the recommendations from the teacher. The teacher is in the position of the person with the most knowledge and passing this on to the student in the form of critique.

The second critique occurs when the student presents their badvert to a peer along with their self evaluation of their learning (Figure 6.4). By considering what the learner has accomplished the peer understands their next learning step. This is a form of peer modelling or teaching, where one student is helping another student to learn.

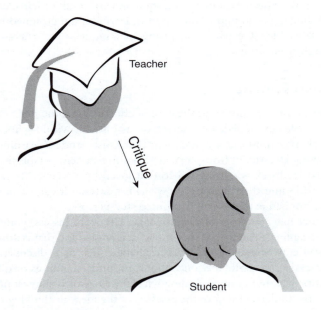

Figure 6.3 Teacher critique.

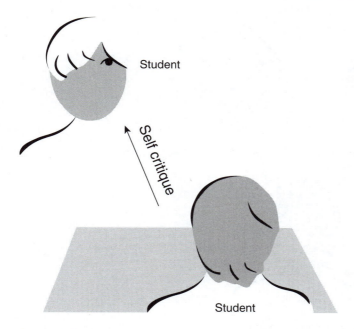

Figure 6.4 Peer critique.

The third critique is when the badvert is shared and considered by both the learner and a peer, an expert, or the teacher. In this case it is the connection between the two participants where the learning occurs. The student and the peer learn collaboratively as they discuss the concepts, skills involved and the outcomes so far. It is through this connection that critical thinking can result in powerful learning and knowledge development (Figure 6.5).

While each critique can lead to learning, it is when the critical thinking involves active dialogue that focuses on learning, concepts and/or skills that knowledge may be created and shared, as illustrated in the third critique. This is more difficult to accomplish than the first two critiques as participants in the dialogue need to have developed a range of critical thinking and dialogic skills if it is to be successful. Skills would include applying different perspectives, listening to critique and building on what is being said or written, persistence, being fair-minded, open and flexible. Such a dialogue would consider the learning against the evaluation criteria, including the negative aspects of the badverts, and the implications and future development of the badvert.

Effective assessment that is used to inform learning processes requires the assessor to understand the thinking processes of the students. Having a student articulate their reasoning or thinking can give the necessary insight for a teacher to identify any misconceptions, learning needs, or why a student is interpreting a concept or skill in a certain way. This knowledge informs the assessment and teaching response. Using this knowledge enables the teacher to be culturally responsive and address the learning needs of the students they teach. For example, if students are learning about sustainability of natural resources, one student may consider this from economic and scientific terms, another may consider it from a

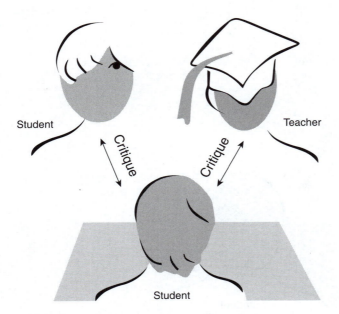

Figure 6.5 Critique for knowledge creation.

perspective of their ancestors and their role as guardians of the land. The teacher can initiate learning about different perspectives of sustainability in a way which does not place greater validity of one over the other.

Evidence of critical thinking can be added to the learner's progress record. Such evidence may reflect conceptual understanding, skill development or learning of an aspect of the curriculum aligned to the underpinning ontological architectural framework.

Summary

Critical thinking is an essential aspect of learning in the digital age when there is a belief that all knowledge is debatable and learners have instant access to information, data and resources. Digital age students learn to be critical consumers of information, able to evaluate the sources and validity of data and resources they access. As well as learning generic critical thinking skills, they also master critical thinking that is specific to a subject discipline. This includes thinking critically about the nature of the subject being studied, and the concepts, skills and methodologies within the subject.

Critical thinking occurs as a student monitors and regulates their learning progress using metacognitive strategies. During this process students compare and evaluate what they are learning with pre-existing understandings, their progress towards learning mastery or knowledge creation, and the strategies they are using for learning. The assessment process can be a positive learning experience when it involves students thinking critically about their learning.

Critical thinking can be a powerful tool for learning and an essential component of knowledge creation. Collaborative critical thinking can add a dimension through the variation of ideas and perspectives that occur through connected diverse learners. Thinking critically, giving and receiving critique, can result in new perspectives or ideas emerging. Learning in the digital age involves thinking critically in a detailed and analytical way.

Chapter 7

Learning in the digital age

In the digital age learning within the schooling system involves mastering concepts and skills, exploring the boundaries of the concepts and skills, and creating and sharing knowledge. Borko and Putnam (1996) offer a succinct definition of learning from a cognitive science perspective which is relevant to a digital age:

> *Learning is an active, constructive process that is heavily influenced by an individual's existing knowledge and beliefs and is situated in particular contexts.*

(pp. 674–675)

This definition has two important implications for learning in the digital age. The first is about the individual and the second is about the role of context. An individual's role in the learning process includes the knowledge they bring, their beliefs and their level of motivation. The context provides the learning environment and the learning experience.

To be active and constructive requires the learner to have a level of agency within the learning process rather than passively sitting listening or reading words of wisdom hoping that they will learn by just being present. This requires motivation, a framework for their learning and metacognitive skills to monitor and evaluate learning progress.

Motivation

Students in the digital age continue to have varying levels of intrinsic and extrinsic motivation. From a psychological perspective a student's intrinsic motivation is stimulated through learning which includes novelty, agency (student choice and control), an appropriate level of difficulty, and is relevant to the learner's knowledge base and interests. Extrinsic motivation can provide a goal which causes a student's learning behaviour to become agentic as they strive to achieve a desired outcome (Ryan and Deci, 2000). Expectancy-value theory highlights the interaction of personal beliefs with the context to determine learner motivation (Atkinson and Raynor, 1974). This theory presents motivation like an outcome which is dependent on a learner's expectations of success and the relative value of that success (Figure 7.1). The expectation of success is influenced by intrinsic motivational aspects and the relative value of success by extrinsic motivators.

If a student is learning to ski with the purpose of being able to go skiing with their friends then the equation may initially look like Figure 7.2.

If after the first day on the slopes the learner has fallen over and not been able to keep up with his friends the motivation to ski may drop dramatically as the novelty is wearing off and

Figure 7.1 Expectancy-value theory.

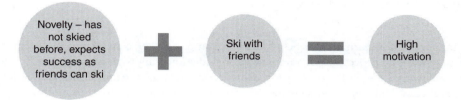

Figure 7.2 Expectancy-value theory of a wannabe skier.

Figure 7.3 Expectancy-value theory of wannabe skier after first day.

the level of difficulty was too advanced for the novice skier. The expectations of learning immediately were not realised. The wannabe skier may give up depending on how much they want to be able to ski with their friends and how much they doubt their ability to learn (Figure 7.3).

To increase motivation the skier will need to have a positive experience at the start of the second day either on an easier slope, with an instructor or group that is at the same level as him or (less likely) to become even more determined to ski with his friends.

There is little reason to believe that the student motivation in the digital age will be different to how it is currently. There have been researchers who have pointed to the use of digital technology as being motivating for students (for example; Passey *et al.*, 2004; Pedretti *et al.*, 1998), but this motivation is attributable to the novelty value or a change in the way that teaching and learning was occurring such as the students being actively involved in learning rather than passive learners (Moss *et al.*, 2002). Roschelle *et al.* (2000) examined how computer technology can be used to motivate learners. Their research found that active engagement, participation in groups, frequent interaction, gaining feedback and connections to real-world contexts enhanced how children learn while using computer-based applications. It appears that it is the pedagogical nuances within the learning experience that are motivational rather than the digital technology per se.

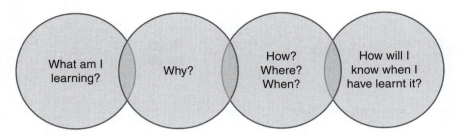

Figure 7.4 Framework for learning.

A framework for learning can help students gain a sense of control and involvement within the learning process. Such a framework includes knowing what is being learnt, how, where and when it will be learnt, why it is being learnt, and how the learner will know when they have learnt it (Figure 7.4). Having a framework for learning is linked to motivation; it can help the learner to identify the relative value of success and give some control and sense of purpose to the student.

Making connections to a student's existing knowledge and experiences underpins the process of learning and would be considered as they contemplate what they are learning. The 'What am I learning?' question should build on their existing knowledge or experiences and the 'How?' should include consideration about how connections are made with prior knowledge.

In a teaching focused system these questions are ones that the teacher considers as part of their planning process; some may share this with the students. In a learning focused system these questions are considered by the students and are central to the learning process. The questions 'Why?' and 'How will I know when I have learnt it?' are likely to have similar answers in a learner focused system. This is not to say that this type of framework should be applied for every small aspect of learning, as to do so would take some of the novelty, variation and excitement out of the learning process. It may also be explored after the student has been introduced to a topic or concept rather than prior to the start of learning.

The question 'What am I learning?' is most powerful when phrased as a question. For example, 'How can I help a hockey goalie improve his or her success rate?' rather than 'I am learning how to train a hockey goalie'; or, 'Was Alexander the Great really great?' rather than 'I am learning why Alexander was considered "great".' Having the core purpose of learning phrased as a question frames knowledge away from a positivist perspective to one that is more open for discovery and creating knowledge as it suggests that there may be multiple answers and critical thinking will be required.

The 'Why?' question establishes the value of learning from a student's perspective and can be linked to participation in society and thus the goal of schooling. Learning about training a hockey goalie may have the purpose of learning how to develop and evaluate training programmes to enable the learner to maximise their own and others' sporting performances. Learning why Alexander was or wasn't great might develop critical thinking and debating skills and create understanding of Macedonian culture, thereby increasing understanding of their own culture.

The digital age promises a range of places where learning can occur. The physical space is not limited to classrooms, library or the desk at home, and perhaps it never was.

However, wireless networks and mobile devices allow access to information and learning environments from any place where there is an Internet connection. This access also influences when learning can occur. In particular, collaborative tasks are not limited to when the learning group is all in the same room, as they can be interacting synchronously or asynchronously online.

Using a framework for learning is an example of a metacognitive tool. Learners in the digital age will develop and use a range of strategies to help them think about and monitor their own learning progress. Frameworks, graphic organisers, rubrics and concept maps are examples of tools that can help students to evaluate the choices and progress they make in their learning. A range of tools can be accessible through the online learning environment for students to explore, use and evaluate. Evaluating learning progress can be through annotated e-portfolios linked to a database of student learning progress. The use of meta-cognition aligns with motivation theory and the idea that students will leave school with the ability to continue to learn independently.

Students of all ages in the digital age have learning experiences that scaffolds their developing understanding of concepts and skills, and guides them towards creating and sharing knowledge beyond the immediate learning environment.

Examples of digital age learning experiences

Learning in the digital age is a process of mastering concepts and skills, exploring the boundaries of these and creating knowledge through connections. A range of examples follow from across subjects and student ages. The examples include: telling a story, poetry, conversations in a foreign language, atoms and molecules, elite performance, urban patterns, artistic messages and 'back to the future'.

Telling a story

Literacy in English gives students access to the understanding, knowledge, and skills they need to participate fully in the social, cultural, political, and economic life of the country in which they live and the wider world. To be successful participants, they need to be effective oral, written and visual communicators who are able to think critically and in depth (Ministry of Education, 2007, p. 18).

This is an example of a learning experience for young children. Prior to being able to read and write, children are able to develop their storytelling skills. Digital technologies enable students to consider the art of storytelling and create their own oral and visual story that can be shared with family or a broader audience.

Initially the students listen to the teacher telling (not reading) the students short stories. The students' learning is scaffolded through discussion and questions to identify the characters and the context of each story and explain how they identified them. Students listen to the same stories again, this time identifying what is included in the beginning, the middle and the end of each story, and consider the concept of structure.

The students listen to the same stories again, which are this time accompanied with a visual representation. The children consider if seeing the image changed what they thought of the characters and the context, and if it did, how. Each student then selects three stories read by a child of the same age and listens to these on their mobile learning devices.

Along with a story told by the teacher in a monotone, muffled and differing tempo voice, the students contemplate what a story teller can do to make their stories interesting.

Each child chooses which story out of all they have heard is their favourite and tells their learning partner about the structure of their favourite story and what they liked or didn't like about the characters, the context and the visual representation. The teacher listens to the discussions and helps any student who has not mastered the concepts of structure, characters and context in a story.

The students then choose who they would like to create a story for. They think about the sort of story that person might like – the type of characters and the context. Then they think about what will happen in their story at the beginning, the middle and the end. They create a visual representation to go with the story. This could be on paper or an electronic rendering on their mobile learning device.

A peer listens to the story to identify the characters, context and the structure, giving feedback to the creator of one thing they like and one suggestion that could make the story better. Then the student explains their story to the teacher, identifying the audience, characters and the context before recording themselves telling the story with an attached visual representation. The stories are uploaded and shared, receiving feedback from a wider audience, such as family.

This learning activity focuses on students developing an understanding of creating and telling stories. It aims to develop metacognitive skills through learning to check for structure, characters and context of a story. The students are scaffolded into using critical thinking and giving feedback to peers which, when applied explicitly in different contexts, can become metacognitive strategies.

This activity aligns with motivation theory in that the student is able to choose the audience for their story and the content of their creation. The level of difficulty can be flexible with the teacher on hand to modify learning to match an appropriate level for the student.

The learning is aligned with digital age theory as the students make connections with their own experiences and knowledge and with their peers as they develop conceptual

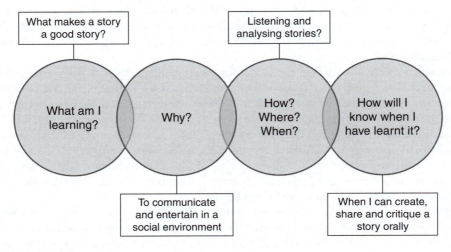

Figure 7.5 Framework for learning storytelling.

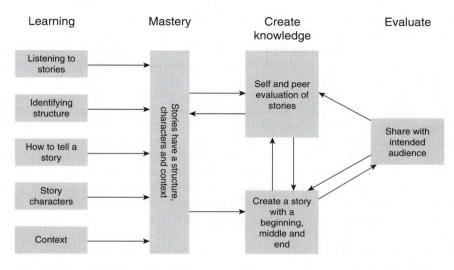

Figure 7.6 Storytelling learning experience model.

understanding. They are scaffolded to attain mastery of the key concepts then they apply the concepts to create and record a story which they critique and share beyond the classroom environment. At this age the critique from beyond the classroom is likely to be positive evaluative encouragement rather than descriptive suggestions on their learning progress. The sharing of exemplar stories from one year to the next may increase the level of learning across the years as the exemplars improve in quality and critique over time.

Poetry

Learning about poetry in the digital age can be an enriching experience that helps to develop or maintain a collaborative learning environment. Learning is structured around some key questions that allow students to explore and co-construct the answers following a discovery learning model.

> By understanding how language works, students are equipped to make appropriate language choices and apply them in a range of contexts. Students learn to deconstruct and critically interrogate texts in order to understand the power of language to enrich and shape their own and others' lives.
>
> (Ministry of Education, 2007, p. 18)

In this learning experience students in groups of three collaborate to support each other. The learning groups are responsible for all members of the group's success in learning about poetry and the creation of a poem. The peers become the people to ask when unsure what to do, they are encouraged to share metacognitive strategies, critique each others' progress towards learning mastery and to support each other in the learning process. The teacher allocates the students into their groups based on their knowledge of the students and the skills they bring. The teacher would have explored each student's learning evidence in the progression database to see what they have already accomplished in the area of poetry. Teaching how to learn collaboratively in small teams is integrated explicitly into the teaching programme as it can take an extended period of time to develop the skills and environment conducive to risk taking, constructive disagreement and effective group based learning (Johnson and Johnson, 2010).

The introduction is a sharing of the goal of learning so that the learners consider and plan how they can get to the end point. The end point is that each of the students will create and share a poem with a specific purpose. The theme may be co-constructed with the class and focus on lyric poetry. As a class the students are guided to decide what they need to learn to accomplish the goal. They could decide that they need to identify what poems they think are good, then explore what features or techniques makes them stand out. This exploration would include a range of learning activities including imaging, where students draw a picture for each stanza of a poem, and the exploration of symbolism in poetry. From this they can develop an evaluation tool and create their own poem ready to share and for critique.

After looking back through their own learning records to revise what they have previously learnt about poetry, students consider 'What is good lyric poetry?' A wide range of poems can be accessed in both the written and oral form through the virtual learning environment which students listen to and look at on their learning management devices using headphones. A number of these poems will include lyrics which are familiar to the students. Others may be from different cultural contexts and a range of well-known poems. The students have to decide which ones they personally like the most and why. They discuss their favourites and reasons within their learning group then each upload the one poem they like the most into the class think space. The group of poems presented in the class think space forms the basis of analysis. As a class they develop a rubric to show what they believe makes an awful poem, an OK poem, a good poem and a great poem, testing the rubric on a number of poems and sharing their interpretations with peers, as poetry can be subjective.

The students consider literary features, underlying rhetoric, images, emotional responses, irony, prosody, form, diction and function, through discussion, interactive learning activities and identifying examples within the selected poems, creating hyperlinks for later reference.

In the students' personal virtual think space they develop a range of examples of literary features, forms and function that they may want to use later when they develop their own poem. Each student uploads a poem they believe is great and explains what makes this a great poem through annotation. The teacher discusses this with each student.

When students think they have learnt features, form and function they take an online computerised adaptive quiz, a quiz which asks students to identify different language features. If they stumble on a question the quiz directs them to further learning activities to master the aspect that they were unsure about before moving on. The teacher monitors each student's progress to encourage, help explain and offer strategies to assist an individual's learning.

The student then independently or with a peer creates a poem with a specific purpose using literary features. They critically evaluate their composition against the rubric they created, an activity which may involve evaluating the rubric. How the poem is to be presented to peers in the class and through an online site is considered, with students trialling different visual and aural presentations and gaining critical feedback from their learning team as to whether it could be considered a good poem given its genre. A further iteration of the poem is created, which could be multimedia in form.

The reworked poems are shared beyond the classroom environment, to gain feedback from a wider audience of the perceived value of the poems in a space that is appropriate for the purpose of the poem. This scenario for learning would depend on the students' choices in the co-construction process.

This learning activity should be motivational as it involves using poetry that is likely to appeal to teenage interests and passions. The class as a group co-construct the approach to learning and there is recognition of diverse tastes that will exist as students express their opinions and preferences. The teacher will be on hand to help students work within a level of difficulty that is appropriate to their understanding of poetry. The purpose that the students choose for the poem they create can provide extrinsic motivation. If they prefer to write a poem with a message about an issue they are passionate about, or a poem about or for a family member, this is likely to be the audience for the feedback.

This is an example of digital age learning as it involves the students making connections with youth culture and their existing knowledge of song lyrics and poems. The students have learnt key concepts within poetry and presentation of poetry for maximum impact. They have applied critical thinking when considering what makes a poem effective (or great) and when considering their own and their peers' poetic creations. They have created original poems and presented these to an appropriate audience and developed these further as they receive feedback from their peers, the teacher and the audience beyond the classroom environment.

The poetry learning activity can be integrated with other learning areas such as music where students create a song using their poetry.

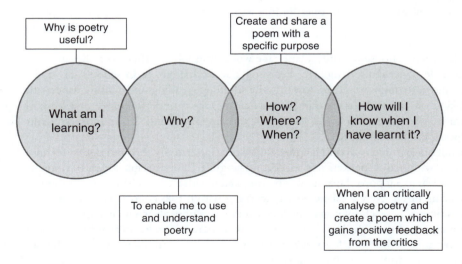

Figure 7.7 Framework for poetry learning experience.

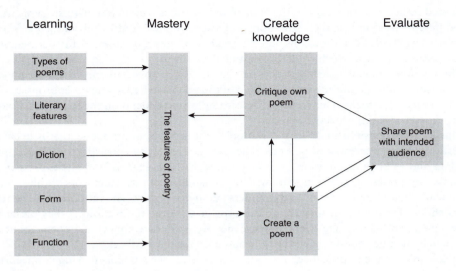

Figure 7.8 Poetry learning experience model.

Language learning

The idea behind this learning scenario can be applied to any level of second language learning.

> Learning a new language extends students' linguistic and cultural understanding and their ability to interact appropriately with other speakers. Interaction in a new language, whether face to face or technologically facilitated, introduces them to new ways of thinking about, questioning, and interpreting the world and their place in it.
> (Ministry of Education, 2007, p. 24)

Students who choose to study a language will commonly say they do so because they want to be able to *speak* the language. Learning a second language in schools has traditionally been more strongly weighted towards the listening, reading and writing aspects than the speaking or spontaneous speaking in particular. This is understandable in a learning environment of one teacher (who can speak the language) and 25 or more students (who cannot speak the language).

Students learning a second language have the opportunity through digital technology to connect with native speakers of their second language. For example a class of students learning English in Sapporo, Japan might be connected with a class of students learning Japanese in Christchurch, New Zealand. If the learning within two cohorts can be loosely aligned across time zones, school years, age levels, and levels of proficiency then both cohorts stand to be enriched through learning about the everyday language and culture of people of a similar age, whether for a few weeks of the year or across a number of years, with opportunities to meet during an exchange process.

Peer tutoring has been found to have both academic and social benefits for both those being tutored and those tutoring (Rohrbeck *et al.*, 2003). The process helps develop metacognition as the tutor explains their thinking processes or models learning to their peer who is learning. In the case of learning a language, the expert will consider the nuances or detail of the language in a way that they may not have thought of before.

If the two groups of students are aged 13 and relative beginners at learning the language the collaborative learning may begin with students being paired with students in the other class on the basis of common interests. These become learning partners and after careful introductory activities to develop the relationships the learning and feedback can begin. Communication can be a regular semi-structured chat time through a synchronous and asynchronous video network.

A regular communication pattern such as once a week may be established, during which time the students videoconference online using language features and vocabulary they have been learning that week followed by social chat. The focus each week could be aligned across the schools and follow national or local events, sporting occasions, movie releases, or aspects of interest to the cohorts of students. Prior to the conversations there could be questions posed so that the students can prepare and gain the necessary vocabulary to communicate. Students will learn to peer tutor their online language learner. As the language and the relationship develops there may be less need for very close alignment between class learning and peer tutoring, as the students will be able to converse with less scaffolding, discuss what they have been learning and things of mutual interest, and critique each other's vocabulary.

A range of teaching and learning activities can occur through the paired students depending on learning needs and interests. For example, one week the two schools may focus on developing 'where is …' and 'what is …'. The students could present pictures or short videos of places that are important to them to their paired learner. Using the language of where the photos are from the language learner asks his or her paired student questions about the places. Synchronous word games could be developed with small groups of learners. Once a range of vocabulary has been learnt in a specific area the students could be given a creative challenge. The pairs of students could be issued bilingual challenges such as collaboratively creating a voiceover animation, a song, story, essay or game. The purpose would be to have the students conversing and getting to understand language and culture through spontaneous conversations.

The development of spontaneous conversation skills is a difficult aspect of language to learn within a traditional classroom setting (Wilson and Starkey, 2009). Language learners benefit from knowing strategies specific to the interactive and unpredictable nature of a conversation. By having spontaneous conversations with native speakers of the language the students may learn to draw on stalling tactics to give them time to compose the next thing to say and they may begin to use their subconscious rather than translating every word back to their first language (Brewer, 2006).

The students in this example should find this type of learning motivating as it aligns with a reason that young people choose to study a language – to be able to understand the native speaker and be able to speak to them. There will be aspects of choice and teen culture brought to the learning. This activity could be hampered if the students flounder with the level of difficulty within the conversations.

The development of the relationship between the learners is an important aspect of this learning activity. Developing a learning relationship with people of the same age should not only help the spontaneous speaking skills, but should also help them understand the culture from a young person's perspective, and as aspects of youth culture tend to follow international trends it is likely that interesting conversations will take place. The students will be developing metacognitive skills as they develop spontaneous speaking skills.

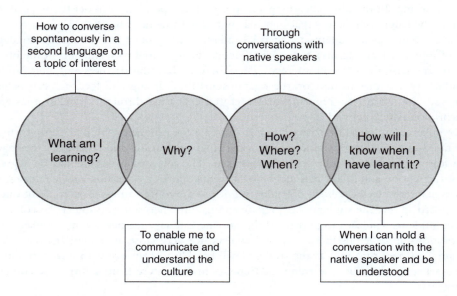

Figure 7.9 Conversation learning experience model.

The digital age holds many exciting opportunities for learning languages, with many developments not yet envisaged. Mobile devices offer a range of applications which can be useful, but I believe will not replace the rich knowledge that is gained from learning about the people and their culture through language. The pairing of language learners for mutual collaborative learning is achievable through fast Internet, video conference technologies, and an intuitive online learning environment. While the main purpose is not to create new knowledge, this may eventuate through the collaborative learning relationships between the students where two cultural perspectives merge (Figure 7.10).

Atoms and molecules

Secondary school students do not always have the opportunity to have a subject specialist teacher in the same physical room as them when they are learning. They may live in a small or isolated community with few teachers or they may not be able to attend school due to health or circumstances. In the digital age these students do not have to learn in isolation from their peers as they can be part of rich learning environments with multiple opportunities for collaborative and supported learning. Developing peer relationships, particularly amongst adolescents, can have a positive influence on learning.

The online learning environments for groups of school students are likely to evolve rapidly during the digital age. It is hard to predict what digital technologies will be available for learners in the future so some assumptions based on current knowledge are made in this scenario. These include:

- All students will have access to a virtual learning environment.
- A virtual learning environment will be intuitive, simple to navigate, and personalised.

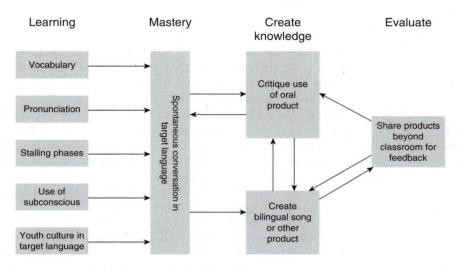

Figure 7.10 Conversation learning experience model.

- Students will not need to carry large devices or learning materials with them as storage will be remote and image projection will not rely on large screens attached to devices.
- Learners will be able to collaborate synchronously with other learners or experts through the learning portal. This will be enhanced by easy access to collaboration tools such as the ability to share and examine information synchronously, built in scheduling with strategic metacognitive guidance, and intuitive links to relevant information. Such collaborations may be through recordable holographic virtual meetings.
- The teacher's portal access gives an immediate view of student learning and the ability to give direct formative feedback to each learner. Any events or lack of learning progress occurring within the environment are red flagged for the relevant teacher's immediate attention and intervention. The online learning environment will be connected to or integrated with a learner management system so that the overall progress of each student's learning is monitored against the targets that have been collaboratively identified between the student, their family and the teachers.

A group of learners who live in different communities may form a cohort of 25 students being taught by a science teacher with an aim to: *develop students' understanding of the world based on current scientific theories* (Ministry of Education, 2007).

Young people are interested in the world around them and why it is how it is. This learning activity aims to use that curiosity and the use of emotional tags to underpin the learning of current theories of atomic structure and molecules.

The human brain gives prominence to memories which are connected to emotional events (Anderson *et al.*, 2006). A learning activity which stirs emotion can aid recollection of both the situation and the ideas embedded within the event. This is a particularly useful learning aid for adolescents for whom interactions with their peers are highly valued and can be emotionally charged.

The learners are (re)introduced to the concept of atomic structure and the periodic table through a range of interactive programmes within the learning environment. The students master understanding about the structure of atoms, how ions are formed and how molecules form by gaining, losing or sharing electrons. Their progress and level of mastery are monitored and feedback given to the students as they are learning. This may be through a computer adaptive programme that links the learners to interactive resources tailored for their needs to help them master the concepts.

The teacher allocates each student a chemical element from across the periodic table. They are to take on the personality of that chemical element as they create a profile in an 'atomic social network'. Their profile will include their structure, likes and dislikes, ambitions, favourite historical events they have been involved in and pictures or video of the atom. During a synchronous meeting each learner introduces themselves as their atom and encourages other atoms to look at their profile. They also outline which other atoms they feel particularly attracted to and what might eventuate if they got together.

The learners explore other atomic profiles developed by their peers and invite atoms to be their 'friends' if they are able to combine to form molecules and through these connections explore types of matter they could form and how. This may involve inviting other atoms to join their discussion. Groups develop around everyday substances, such as silica, oxygen, sodium and calcium, which form the window (or glass) group. Each group develops and presents a multimedia dramatisation to illustrate the role each plays in making up the matter identified. This latter activity is likely to encompass emotional input and therefore be memorable for the students.

There is a danger that learners could focus on completing the activities more than the learning function. The learner framework in this activity provides a metacognitive function with an explicit overview between the learning and the tasks. The learning framework for this activity is outlined in Figure 7.11.

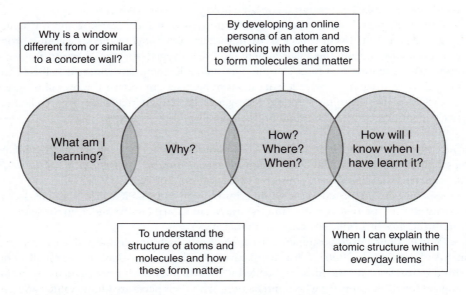

Figure 7.11 Framework for learning experience, atoms and molecules.

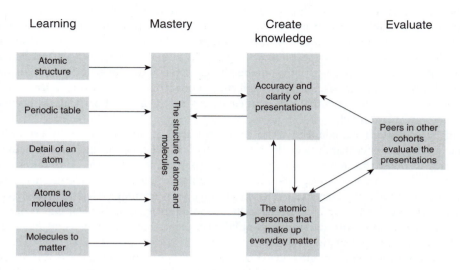

Figure 7.12 Atoms and molecules learning experience model.

The learning focus is linked to the broad educational aim of students leaving school and contributing to society knowledgably by understanding the world in which they live. It is structured around learning in the digital age by being underpinned by connectivist and motivational learning theory. There is a novelty factor in the students taking on the persona of a particular atom and interacting with peers using this persona. The use of social networking is a feature of youth culture and the development of relationships with peers through this learning activity is likely to enhance the collaboration within the learning environment.

The presentations will be self and peer evaluated for clarity and accuracy. They can also remain within the learning environment as exemplars or as a resource for future students learning about atoms and molecules who may identify ways to modify or expand them.

Elite performance

Physical education students in their senior years learn about physiology and sports coaching, and more specifically the concept of effective training for improved performance and mastering specific coaching skills which integrate the use of digital technology.

> In physical education, the focus is on movement and its contribution to the development of individuals and communities. By learning in, through, and about movement, students gain an understanding that movement is integral to human expression and that it can contribute to people's pleasure and enhance their lives.
>
> (Ministry of Education, 2007, p. 23)

The idea for this learning activity came from observing and discussing teaching in the digital age with a highly competent beginning teacher as part of a doctoral study (Starkey, 2010).

The teacher introduces the topic of study through an activity where students have to perform a measurable sporting movement. They then contemplate and discuss how they could improve their performance. The explicit purpose is to increase the students' expectancy value of the learning they will be focusing on. To raise the expectation of success the process of learning is explained by outlining the concepts and skills to be mastered, the critique learners will undertake, how they will create knowledge, and how their learning will be evaluated by the students themselves, their peers, the teacher and participants beyond the classroom environment.

Initially students make connections to previous learning and knowledge by exploring interactive programmes that explain physiology such as muscle function and bone structure. The students revise through an online mastery test to check their knowledge of terms and concepts. The programme is adaptive in that it recognises when a student has not mastered a concept and guides the learner to a relevant video clip and learning activity. The results of student progress of learning are automatically linked to their record of learning progress and their teacher works with the students until they have mastered the knowledge they need to apply to a coaching scenario.

As a group the students are introduced to a range of digital tools that are used in sports coaching, which could include motion capture software through which the detail of physiological movement within a sport can be analysed and a participatory three dimensional virtual reality programme to guide body movement and develop specific skills. The students learn collaboratively in groups of three to explore the use of the technology to ascertain how it can be used to improve sporting performance within a sport that they play. This learning activity is scaffolded by the teacher and occurs in a flexible learning space or in the community where the technology is available. By the end of this activity the teacher will have assessed whether each student has gained an understanding of coaching skill development for sports performance and how this can be achieved using digital technology.

Each student finds a client, which can be a classmate, who they will coach in a sport they are familiar with (anything from croquet to rugby). Initially they discuss with their client which skill aspects of their performance they would like to improve. The student discusses the client's preferences with their teacher and receives guidance on suitability and level of difficulty of developing a training schedule for the identified aspects.

The student will investigate and learn about the relevant physiology involved in this aspect of the sport, record their client's current style or performance using motion capture software then develop a training programme based on the physiological understanding, drawing on their knowledge of physiology, the sport being played, and existing training programmes, some of which may have been developed by previous students of physical education. The training schedule will be peer critiqued and the teacher and an expert coach from the identified sport will give advice and guidance prior to implementation. The implementation of the training schedule will include regular evaluations of client progress. The training plan and progress of each client would be shared and compared through an online learning network where critique and suggestions from other students or sports experts will inform tweaks and changes made to the programme. The clients would be identified with pseudonyms online to prevent any potential embarrassment. At the conclusion the student critically evaluates his or her learning of physiology, the implementation of training programmes and the use of tools within sports coaching.

Figure 7.13 outlines a framework that can help students structure their learning for this topic. The design of the learning activity is cognisant of motivational theory in that it allows

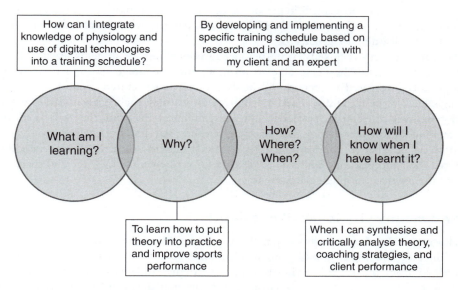

Figure 7.13 Sports coaching framework for learning.

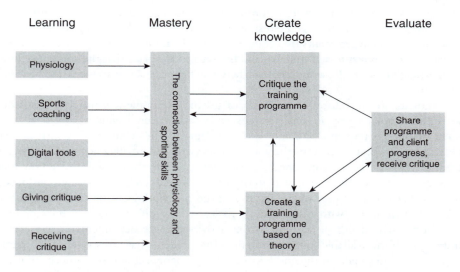

Figure 7.14 Sports coaching learning experience model.

for personal choice and links to student knowledge and interests (the sport they play). Having a choice gives a sense of agency in the learning and can increase the perceived value of success. The teacher would provide the level of guidance necessary for each student through the learning process to ensure that the choices they make are at an appropriate level of difficulty. The learner chooses the client they are going to coach. The time spent with the client when there is improvement in performance could be a strongly rewarding experience for both the student and the client. It is likely to involve emotional connections which can strengthen the learning experience.

The learning focus is linked to the broad educational aim of students leaving school contributing to society by being able to promote and encourage sporting performance through coaching based on theoretical knowledge. It is structured around learning in the digital age by being underpinned by connectivist learning theory. Each learner will be developing their conceptual knowledge and skills, and more than this, they will be critiquing, creating knowledge, sharing their learning beyond the classroom environment to gain feedback on their ideas. The learning does not end when the student has understood or mastered the concepts, they continue to develop ideas to create knowledge and share this beyond the physical learning environment.

Why does my city looks like it does?

This learning activity was developed initially by a geography teacher aiming to integrate the use of digital technologies into his students' learning and at the same time move the focus of learning from the teacher giving information to the students constructing learning (Starkey and McCarthy, 2008). It has been further developed with the future technologies in mind.

Geography students explore the complex processes that shape cultural environments which change over time, vary in scale and from place to place, and create spatial patterns (Ministry of Education, 2007). To help students to understand the concept of spatial variation within urban environments two contexts are studied. One is the local context which is familiar and of interest to the students and the second is a place that the students choose from anywhere in the world, assuming that there will be ready access to maps and historical information.

The students are introduced to the idea of urban development through a simulation game, which students play in small groups with each group having the role of town planners of one area within a rapidly growing region. The game begins with a small number of local people in each of the allocated sites and potentially ends with cities. The different groups can collaborate, specialise or compete. The students consider how their city has changed over time, spatial patterns that emerged such as housing, businesses, transport, what decisions they made that did or did not work as planned. They compare their city and decisions with other groups to learn how different and similar patterns might emerge. The depth of learning in this activity may be dependent on the level of sophistication of the available software, the time that students have to spend on this game, and the explicit links made at the end between their experiences and the concept of urban spatial patterns.

To develop further understanding of the concepts the students explore a specific area of their city to identify characteristics of the area, history, function and demographics. The students work in learning teams using statistical data, historical information and council zoning information. They visit their designated area to talk with people and to create a visual record. The findings are analysed and synthesised, then integrated into an open access interactive map of the city. Other students from following years or different local schools can further develop the findings and add information about other areas of the city.

The findings may be critiqued and used by the local council who could be consulted on an annual focus for interviews.

After considering the city as a whole, the students then research a city of their choice to identify urban spatial patterns and how these have been influenced by culture, politics, economics and natural forces. This may give further insight into the uniqueness of their own city, which may lead to further critique and amendments of the evolving interactive map.

The learning could include a *what if* thinking activity to consider the future of urban spatial patterns – for example, what would happen if public transport were the only option available for the citizens (if private cars were banned)? This could be investigated through the simulation game, connecting the students' learning from the start of the sequence to the end.

In this example the learning framework could be split into three different aspects of learning – one for the simulation activity, one for the research of the students' own city and one for the city of the students' choice. Figure 7.15 is a learning framework which includes the three activities which all explore the same concepts.

The students are learning about the world in which they live and considering how the world might be in the future. They are not only learning about the patterns in their urban context, but they are also developing knowledge that they are sharing with an audience that is beyond the classroom. Each year students develop this knowledge further rather than 'rediscover' what is already known.

The students in this activity are actively creating local knowledge which is shared and further developed over time and by different geography students. Collaboration with local urban designers would reinforce the value of the knowledge being created. The students are actively involved in the learning, with a focus on their local environment and choice of overseas city which should stimulate their interest. Creating knowledge and sharing this

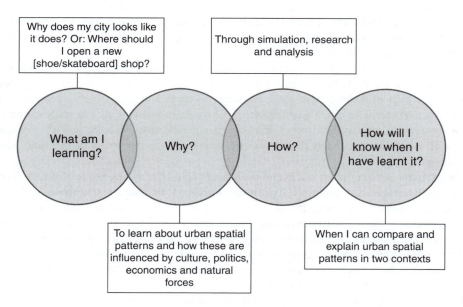

Figure 7.15 Urban spatial patterns framework for learning.

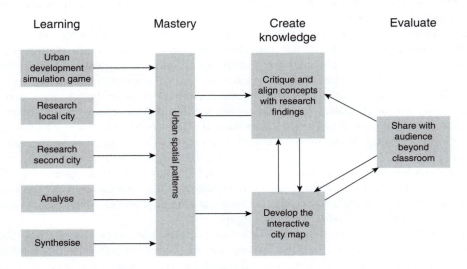

Figure 7.16 Urban spatial patterns learning experience model.

beyond the classroom environment with other students and the local council is an example of how learning theory in the digital age can be put into practice.

Artistic messages

Citizens taking an active role in society may find a time when they have a message that they want others to consider about something that is happening that they do not agree with. This message can be shared through the arts – connecting social change with poetry, painting, movies, animation or song.

This activity integrates learning in the arts with social studies, drawing on two bodies of knowledge. Initially students are shown and listen to works of art that are from a protest movement which is likely to have some relevance to them and they discuss their reaction to those art works. They then learn about the protest movement that is represented in the works of art; the issue, context, participants, perspectives, events, and the agentic forces. This provides a context to explore the messages that the artists of the time were presenting.

The students explore the art works and the artists behind the works. Some of the students may be studying visual art and explore paintings, looking at techniques, symbolism and style used to make an impact. They may be able to listen to interviews or find exhibition notes about the artist's ideas at the time of painting. A student studying music may do the same exploration with protest songs, or the student of English can explore poetry or the film student could explore how a documentary maker created a short film with a message of social change. The learner will make connections between the protest movement and the artist and works of art within the movement.

A contemporary issue of the students' choosing, something they feel passionate about, is examined as a comparison and to broaden understanding of the concept of art to convey a message of protest. This could be about human rights, equity, cultural extinction, global warming, war, rights of young people, sustainability, etc. As a cohort the group explores the issue by examining the context, participants, perspectives, events, and the agentic forces. They explore possible outcomes within different scenarios.

Each student then creates an art work with a message to encourage a target audience to think about the issue the class has explored, drawing on their emerging knowledge about the issue and protest art. The resulting art works are displayed as a cohesive multimedia exhibition. Such an exhibition could be presented in a virtual space, shared with the art network, and it could also be presented in a physical exhibition. The combining of poetry, song, documentary, graphic images and painting could provoke a strong emotional response from the wider audience. The learning framework for this activity is outlined in Figure 7.17.

Motivational aspects of this learning activity include making connections to an issue that is relevant to the students; the authentic purpose of the learning; to get a meaning across to an audience. The learning within this activity has the possibility of creating a class of social activist artists.

Learning about social change through artistic creations is relevant to learning in the digital age. Students learn how to access information and discuss subjects through the Internet. They are able to exhibit their own creations cohesively through an online portal, raising awareness and participating in social change, even if only in a small way.

Back to the future

This example was originally developed for an integrated programme for online distance students aged 12 to 14 years.[1] Before joining the programme the students were asked what they wanted to know about themselves, their local environment and the world. One theme that emerged from their answers was that they wanted to know what the future would

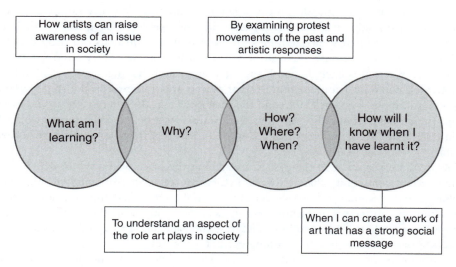

Figure 7.17 Artistic message learning framework.

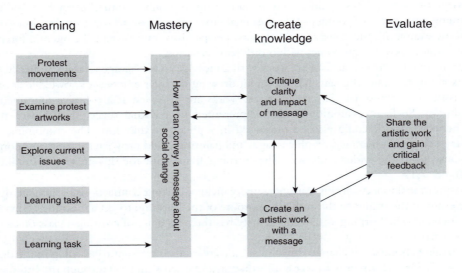

Figure 7.18 Artistic messages learning experience model.

be like. A team of teachers, each with different curriculum expertise, collaborated to develop an integrated topic to guide student learning as they explore what the future would be like.

The learners begin by considering what life was like 50 years ago and what societal and technological changes were anticipated. There are three aspects to exploring the past. The first is interviewing someone who was living 50 years ago to find out how society was different. This has a personal learning focus as the student is likely to choose someone they know well such as a grandparent or a family friend and the conversation is likely to enrich the relationship that the student has with the person being interviewed. If the student struggles to find someone they know who is at least 60 years old there could be a member of the school staff who will be willing to be interviewed. A positive outcome of such a connection is likely for both the interviewer and the interviewee. The focus of the interview could be a combination of what aspects are of interest to the students (such as sports, transport, teen social life) and the memories that the interviewee would like to share. The students could also ask what their interviewee believed the future would be like and the types of technologies that are around today that they would not have believed possible.

The second exploration of the past is researching the place where the students live to examine how a community changes over 50 years. Aspects examined could include demographics, communication technology, transport, social events, food and nutrition, fashion, sports, movies, businesses and employers, music, technologies in the home, household income and spending, and schooling. Pictures, clips and findings could be collated and shared and discussed through the learning portal for the class.

The third exploration is the genre of science fiction. Students are introduced to science fiction with movie or television clips, where they seek to identify the ideas about the future that the creators were identifying. The learners explore the types of technology that were thought could be available in the future, changes in society, and the types of scientific advances anticipated. Learners critique the ideas, noting those which did eventuate and those which have not (or not yet) been adopted. The students read science fiction stories created in the past, analyse and critique these. The purpose is to learn what is involved in the science fiction genre, and what was thought of as 'futuristic' when the story was created. The results from the interviews, research and study of science fiction are shared across the class to summarise the knowledge base of society 50 years ago and to identify how the future was perceived in the past.

From the findings about the past the students consider what the future may be like. They consider what their community will be like based on statistical demographics and the scale of change over the past 50 years. This includes changes to aspects such as communication technology, transport, social events, food and nutrition, fashion, sports, movies, businesses and employers, music, technologies in the home, household income and spending, and schooling. For each change they identify there are likely to be wider implications for society; for example, if they believe that city transport will be airborne this will change the function or perhaps existence of roads. They consider what issues may arise as society changes and technology develops and the types of solutions that could be available. Each student considers what their life might be like in 50 years' time and how they would participate in the society they have identified.

In a small learning team the students explore one scientific development which could be important in the future, such as genetic modification, fuels other than fossil fuels, sustainable energy sources, medical advances such as those which increase human life expectancy, cloning or space exploration.

The ultimate activity in this study is for each student to write a short story in the science fiction genre. The context is their community and the setting is 50 years in the future. Each idea must be justified by the research they have carried out. The short stories are peer edited and critiqued before being published as an electronic book sold through Amazon.com (or similar online retail outlet) with any profits made donated to a group that is working on an issue that the students identified as a concern in their studies.

Students may also critique current science fiction films for how accurate they believe their portrayal of the future is. This could be done through a social network film critique site.

This learning activity has the potential to include all curriculum areas. Home economics students can explore the range of food available and the nutritional difficulties in the past and compare this with the present and consider how it may be in the future. Mathematicians and economists could consider inflation and investments over 50 years. Scientists could consider what scientific advances have been made in the past 50 years and what are likely to occur in the next 50 years. English students will develop an understanding of the science fiction genre and writing short stories for publication. Social scientists will be examining social change, maybe considering what the responsibilities of a citizen were and who made community based decisions in the past, how this compares to the present, and how this may be in the future. Physical education students may be considering how and why a particular sport has changed over time, how it may change in the future and how people may keep their bodies healthy in the future.

This unit of learning is likely to be motivating for the students as it includes choice, is centred around their own lives and has a final product that is shared beyond the classroom with a potentially global audience. An underpinning theme is that the students will not be

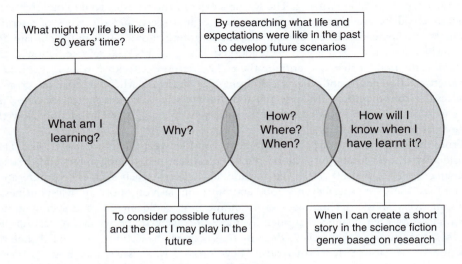

Figure 7.19 Back to the future learning framework.

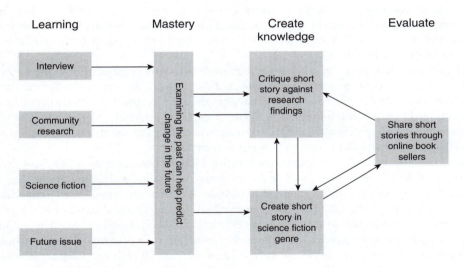

Figure 7.20 Back to the future learning experience model.

passively waiting for changes to occur in the future, but they can be actively involved in shaping their future and the future of their community.

Summary

Learning in the digital age is not a passive activity. Students are actively participating in the process and have some accountability for their own and their peers' learning. With a substantial evidence portfolio available through the learning progress database both the teacher and the student can review what the student has learnt and accomplished in prior years before beginning a learning experience.

A framework for learning tied to motivational theory guided the examples with the aim of increasing students' perceived value of learning and likelihood of success. The learning experiences described focus on students mastering concepts and skills, learning through connections, applying critical thinking, creating knowledge, and sharing learning beyond the learning environment. Each student will receive feedback and will be evaluated by the teacher as to whether mastery level has been reached, knowledge created, or learning shared beyond the context. The learning will be recorded in the student learning progress database with links to the evidence of learning. This may be the topic of discussion and moderation through teacher networks.

Chapter 8

Teaching in the digital age

Effective teaching in the digital age requires a high level of professional knowledge and skill. The teacher needs to be able to recognise what students know and don't know, draw on discipline knowledge, pedagogical content knowledge, educational psychology and knowledge of the context to teach the students concepts and skills that they will need to participate in society. They also need to facilitate opportunities for students to collaboratively create and critique knowledge within and beyond the formal learning environment. Teaching will be a highly skilled and demanding profession (Figure 8.1).

Prioritising teaching or learning

In the digital age teachers will prioritise student learning over teaching. There is a subtle but important difference between teacher decisions which prioritise teaching above learning and those which prioritise learning over teaching. They are two perspectives; both value teaching and learning, but they approach the teaching process from different priorities. The former is to keep the students engaged through the use of resources and carefully designed lessons, the latter is to monitor student learning through use of formative assessment and base teaching decisions on the learning progress of the students.

A teacher who prioritises teaching carefully selects resources and teaching tasks that will disseminate content information for the students to learn. Their classes may be engaged in learning tasks and focused on getting the work done. It is likely that students are directed to ensure they have the correct notes and achievement is measured through task completion. A student who follows the instructions and completes their work (the set tasks) is considered a good student. The teacher may plan in a sequence so that students are being scaffolded through learning tasks as per constructivist learning theory. The teacher may assess to ensure that students have achieved the 'learning intention' that the teacher has shared with the students. Knowledge creation may be shared through movies showing students' art works, poetry written by students, stories or the results of scientific inquiries. The purpose is to showcase what the students have been doing, rather than to extend the learning. It is underpinned by the focus on task goals and task completion rather than the learning. When it does show the learning it is within the framework of 'we are learning about', which tends to be what the teacher is teaching.

A teacher educator or mentor who prioritises teaching over learning will expect to observe clear structured planning, behaviour management that ensures students can focus on the tasks set by the teacher and students who clearly understand what they have to do and when. An outcomes based curriculum that specifies what students need to be able to achieve at certain stages can encourage or underpin prioritising teaching over learning.

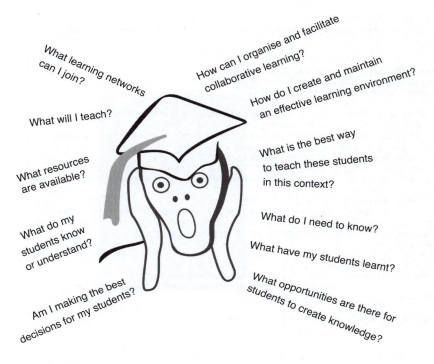

What learning networks can I join?

How can I organise and facilitate collaborative learning?

How do I create and maintain an effective learning environment?

What will I teach?

What is the best way to teach these students in this context?

What resources are available?

What do I need to know?

What do my students know or understand?

What have my students learnt?

Am I making the best decisions for my students?

What opportunities are there for students to create knowledge?

Figure 8.1 The teacher scream.

A teacher who prioritises learning requires similar skills to the teacher who prioritises teaching, but frames their thinking about the process from the perspective of the student rather than the teacher. Their starting point when considering how to teach is the students and their learning needs. The focus is less on getting work done and more on learning. At the end of a formal lesson the students may have nothing physical to show the teacher, but they should be able to explain what they have learnt. A student who demonstrates conceptual understanding, uses critical thought, collaboration, metacognition, and creativity within the subject context is considered a successful learner. The teacher may plan a sequence of learning experiences to scaffold students, assessing their progress along the way and adapting instruction and feedback for individuals or groups of students. They will also encourage students to use the concepts they have learnt creatively, collaboratively and critically.

A teacher educator or mentor who prioritises student learning over behavioural aspects of teaching will expect to observe a learning environment in which the articulation of thought processes, discussions about what is being learnt and a teacher who is focused on understanding the learning that is occurring by individuals and groups.

Pedagogical reasoning

Pedagogical reasoning is the process a teacher undertakes when making teaching decisions prior to, during, and after their students' learning episodes. Lee Shulman's (1987) model of

---

Model of teacher pedagogical reasoning and action for the digital age

(adapted from Shulman, 1987)

Comprehension of subject (content knowledge) including:
- substantive knowledge (concepts and principles); and
- syntactic knowledge (subject methodologies).

Enabling connections – preparation for teaching (pedagogical content knowledge) including:
- reviewing and analysis of student learning records;
- selecting appropriate resources and methods to enable students to make connections between prior knowledge and developing subject knowledge and skills;
- transforming existing knowledge into teachable content;
- enabling opportunities for students to create, critique and share knowledge;
- enabling connections between groups and individuals to develop knowledge of the subject.

Teaching and learning – (knowledge of context) including:
- ongoing evaluation of student learning with feedback to, and discussion with, the students and modification of the teaching process and learning experience where appropriate;
- adaptation and tailoring learning experiences for the students being taught;
- being culturally responsive.

Reflection – (teacher professional learning) including:
- reviewing and critically analysing teaching decisions based on evidence;
- formal and informal professional discussions about student learning, evidence and teaching decisions.

New comprehensions – about the subject, student learning and teaching.

Figure 8.2 Pedagogical reasoning and action in the digital age.

pedagogical reasoning and action was designed to identify the professional practice of teaching that was specific to teachers. The model comprises actions that a teacher undergoes during the teaching process including: comprehension of subject knowledge, transformation of subject knowledge into teachable representations, instruction, evaluation of students' learning and teacher's performance, reflection, and new comprehensions (by the teacher). The underlying purpose of teaching in this model was to impart knowledge to students and then assess them to ensure that they had learnt the intended information, skills or concepts. This model was a useful representation at the time it was published, helping to establish recognition for teaching as professional practice.

Figure 8.2 is a simplified model of pedagogical reasoning in the digital age which prioritises student learning. An earlier version of this was published in 2010 (Starkey, 2010a, p. 243). In the digital age student learning is the focus of teaching decisions.

Teachers draw on knowledge and experience when making teaching decisions. At the planning stage the teacher will draw on their academic knowledge of the subject being taught, pedagogical content knowledge, curriculum, knowledge of the context and learners being taught.

Content knowledge

For a teacher to teach students about a subject they need to be able to draw on their own personal substantive knowledge of the subject gained through academic study.

The substantive knowledge of subject includes the concepts, principles and the nature of the subject. Each subject has a body of knowledge that has been debated and developed over time, evolving as new connections and ideas become embedded. Students in the digital age will continue to learn what each subject contributes to broader understanding of society, the world and beyond, and the methodologies unique to the subject. The more complex the concepts, principles and methodologies being learnt, the greater the level of academic knowledge the teacher requires.

Students learning the social sciences will learn how research, critique, debate and referencing occurs along with key concepts and perspectives. All this knowledge is embedded within the subject and the teacher needs to be able to draw on the substantive knowledge of the subject when making decisions about which aspects to teach, how and why.

Pedagogical content knowledge

Academic knowledge is the basis for the development of a teacher's pedagogical content knowledge, which is essential for effective teaching practice. Pedagogical content knowledge was identified by Lee Shulman (1986) as the understanding and skill needed to teach students the substantive knowledge of a particular subject. It is how to teach a particular concept, methodology or principle based on how students learn, the context, and the resources at hand. For example, a geography teacher needs the substantive knowledge of how natural and cultural processes occur and interact to form the environment in which the students they teach live. They also have the pedagogical content knowledge to inform how they teach the students about their environment, when to use field assignments and the appropriate methodologies for learning beyond the classroom, what models or simulations will help students learn about the processes, how many examples should be used, when to use collaborative learning, when to introduce independent learning tasks and how to familiarise the students with geographic vocabulary and concepts.

Pedagogical content knowledge is important for effective teaching. To teach 6-year-olds how to add the teacher needs to know more than the substantive knowledge (how to add). He or she needs to know the process of *learning* to add and the teaching methods that enable the learner to learn. Likewise the geography teacher may know how the environment has formed through natural and cultural processes, but this alone does not make them an effective teacher. An effective teacher will be able to select appropriate resources and teaching strategies to enable the students to master the concepts, skills and methodologies specific to the subject and design opportunities for students to critique, create and share knowledge.

Professional learning in teaching has been studied and considered over time with different ways of measuring effectiveness suggested. It can be evaluated by how much the teacher enjoyed a professional learning programme, the results of which may depend on the intrapersonal skills of the programme leader, the quality of the lunch or the ease of parking. It may be measured by a behaviourist approach to learning by examining the change in teacher behaviour as a result of the programme. Another way suggested by Kirkpatrick (1994) is to examine the effect on student learning as a result of the programme. A programme that focuses on pedagogical content knowledge is more likely to directly influence student learning than programmes that focus on other aspects of the teaching process.

What is to be taught is guided by a national, regional, district or school-based curriculum. In the digital age teachers will be likely to continue to need knowledge of the curriculum they are to follow, though the nature of the curriculum may be different. This is explored further in the next chapter.

Knowledge of educational psychology

A teacher in the digital age will draw on their knowledge of educational psychology when making teaching decisions. They will understand motivational and behavioural theories and be able to apply appropriate strategies to engage students in learning. For example, an awareness of value-expectancy theory can be applied to teaching when introducing a learning unit by making the learning relevant to the lives of the students. If the students can recognise the value of what they are learning they will be more motivated to apply metacognitive strategies to monitor their own progress and ensure their success. A digital age teacher will make the learning the focus rather than the task. In the poetry learning unit described in the previous chapter the teacher would be emphasising how the use of literary techniques once learnt can be applied to poetry, song lyrics and other literary endeavours. This is a different focus to emphasising the task, the writing of a poem. A teacher who has a strong learning relationship with their students will establish where their interests and motivations lie and use this to help the learner to make connections between their learning and their life. Value-expectancy theory recognises that learners balance the value placed on learning with their expectation of success. If learning something such as how to use literary techniques to write original song lyrics is considered high value in teen culture then the high level of motivation will allow the students who may doubt they are able to develop their literary skills to persevere and the teacher can continue to set challenging learning tasks. If students see little value in learning literary techniques and the task appears daunting, a simpler achievable learning goal would be necessary to motivate the students. Therefore the skilled teacher needs to recognise the level of difficulty and scaffolding that will challenge the learner without demotivating them, which balances the value they place on the learning with their expectation of success (Figure 8.3).

In an ideal world the students would place a high value on every learning focus. In reality not all concepts or skills that students need to learn to participate effectively in society are

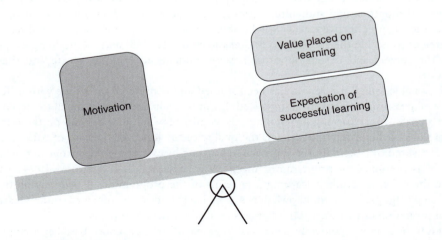

Figure 8.3 Value-expectancy theory.

highly valued by all learners. A challenge for the digital age teacher is to maximise the students' perceived value of learning through making explicit connections between the learning and the students' participation in society. The teacher who can maximise the perceived value of the learning will be able to place greater learning challenges before the students.

An understanding of how memory works can inform teaching decisions. A teacher can incorporate learning activities which require students to become emotionally involved in the learning. This can be useful when learning aspects which require memorisation. This type of learning activity in which students can apply creativity and individual preferences will be remembered long after they have moved on from this class, especially if the students had become emotionally involved in developing their business. Emotional memory tags are thought to help students, particularly young adults, to remember situations and can be useful in education (Richter-Levin and Akirav, 2003).

Teachers are familiar with behavioural theories including the use of extrinsic and intrinsic rewards, behaviour management strategies, and group learning theories. To effectively apply motivational and behavioural theories the teacher establishes and maintains a learning relationship with their students.

Knowledge of learners

The teacher is the adult and mentor in the learning relationship and therefore has the leadership role, responsibility and accountability for their students' learning. By drawing on educational psychology, behaviour management strategies and a focus on developing an effective learning environment, the digital age teacher will develop the learning relationship with each student.

Developing a learning relationship involves not only accessing the learning history of the students being taught it also involves building trust and an understanding of the interests and motivations of the learners. Such a relationship develops through the learning process as the students see the teacher taking an interest in their individual learning needs and giving feedback on how they can progress their understanding of concepts and skills.

There are many aspects to recognising and teaching diverse learners. Students each have one or multiple identity, culture and language which reflects their experiences and the context in which they live. From their families they will have had particular perspectives, values, behaviours, and principles instilled. In diverse societies there can be considerable variation within each cohort of students. It is a challenging task for a teacher to have all their students developing understanding of the concepts being taught when they have diverse funds of knowledge (Hogg, 2010). The learning relationship with students and their families can provide the knowledge the teacher needs to be able to teach and respond to diversity amongst learners.

A student's culture, identity and language are important to how they approach and value school learning. Students are able to make connections between learning and their participation in society when they can see that their identity and culture is respected and understood (Ministry of Education, 2008). While students may have multiple identities that they draw on, particularly during adolescence, the skilled teacher is able to acknowledge and reflect consideration of these through the teaching and learning process.

Contextual knowledge

Pedagogical decisions will be informed by knowledge of the context in which the learner is situated and where the teaching occurs. In the digital age the context may be broader than the local physical environment; it could include a virtual or global environment. Learners may not be situated in the same physical location as the teacher, in which case the context for the teaching and learning may be an online environment. A context is made up of resources, policies, procedures, goals, culture, identity and language(s).

Each context has access to resources which can be used for teaching and learning. This includes people and places in the local community, books, libraries, educational resources such as posters, blocks and models. Through the Internet, people and programmes can be accessed and used as teaching or learning resources. Computerised adaptive learning programmes that guide learning according to student responses to tasks can be useful learning resources especially when data on student learning progress is linked to learning records.

The types of educational digital resources that will become available to teachers and their students are difficult to predict, but it is likely that there will be exponential growth in the range as technologies advance. There is scope for simulation and virtual learning environments to be available to help students learn concepts and skills, and to enable collaboration and evaluation. Such an exponential growth in accessibility and affordability of digital resources may be perceived as making the job of teaching easier. But the digital age teacher will be evaluating each resource to consider whether it will be the best tool to use for the learners and the teaching aims. Selecting and using appropriate learning tools from a wider range may make the job of teaching more complex rather than easier, although it is likely that teachers will share knowledge and experiences through their professional teacher networks.

The context of teaching and learning will be guided by policies and procedures. There will be procedures or ways of doing things for that particular context whether a physical or a virtual context. A teacher or student who changes from one school to another will find that there are differences between the schools and it can take a while to learn the unique way that things are done in a particular context.

Policies are set at a school through to national level. A school will have policies that the teacher is expected to follow in the teaching process. National policies such as accreditation requirements for teaching, the gathering of evidence of student learning or achievement, examinations and attendance, will all be taken into consideration by the teacher when making decisions about their teaching and their students' learning.

Along with policies and procedures there may be internal or external goals that have been set that informs decisions that teachers make. If a school has set a goal to have all the students creating knowledge in at least one subject per term, or a national goal is for learning to be bilingual, then the teacher will be considering how to incorporate these goals within their teaching plans.

The way that things are done in a particular learning environment reflects the culture of the context. The way that people are greeted, how they participate, behavioural expectations, hierarchical systems, how feedback is given, and the language(s) used are all aspects of the culture of the learning environment. The teacher has an important role in setting the cultural context of the learning environment and establishing the contextual identity. In the digital age students bring their own culture, identity and language to the learning environment and the teacher will take this into account as they make teaching decisions.

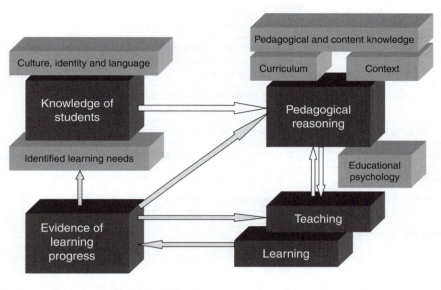

☐☐☐▷ = Critical analysis and evaluation

Figure 8.4 Evidence based teaching practice.

Evidence of learning progress

In the digital age the teacher uses evidence to understand the learning needs of the students being taught (Figure 8.4). The development of technologies or software to record, analyse and report on student learning progress is likely to provide valuable information for teachers. Student information can be the basis of teaching plans that will progress student learning across years at school. Each student's learning history contained within the data system will be cumulative over the learner's schooling with each teacher contributing to the record and linking learning to evidence. As a teacher is allocated learners, they are able to explore their students' learning achievements through the data system, compare their progress over the years with others in the cohort, pinpoint their learning strengths and aspects they have progressed slowly with, and identify the context or focus of studies. Accessing a groups' rich learning data to explore patterns across a cohort can inform teaching plans that focus on the learning needs of the specific students being taught.

Teaching for mastery learning

The teaching process in the digital age will prioritise learning over tasks. A range of teaching strategies will be used in the digital age, some of which may not yet be developed or named, but each will focus on student learning. Figure 8.5 outlines types of learning focus and the associated strategies.

It is important to master the skills and concepts so that they are thoroughly understood and embedded in the mental schema to be drawn upon and used as knowledge artefacts at appropriate times. Mastery level for concepts can be considered within the context of the

	Examples of learning experiences
Conceptual understanding	Simulation, direct instruction, using models or graphical organisers, interactive programmes, experiments, field research, modelling
Concept mastery	Inquiry or research, collaborative learning, questioning, game or quiz development, peer teaching
Skills introduction	Modelling, simulation, virtual reality
Skills mastery	Coaching, competition, peer teaching
Critical thinking	Problem solving, simulations, debating, questioning
Creation of knowledge	Problem solving, collaboration, mashing

Figure 8.5 Learning experiences.

SOLO taxonomy (Biggs and Collis, 1982). A student may start learning the individual parts of a concept (prestructural stage of SOLO taxonomy). For example, if students are learning the concept of sustainability they may start by learning about mining and oil extraction through an interactive educational programme with embedded video footage. From there the teacher can teach about the limitations of the use of these resources through an interactive timescale programme, thus the students will be reaching the unistructural stage of the SOLO taxonomy where simple and obvious connections are made, but their significance may not be grasped. The students may then consider their household consumption over a week, what is brought into the household and what leaves. This could be recorded by scanning each product entering the house and mashing with the online energy consumption figures for the household. Analysis can be provided through a sustainability website. This takes the students to a multistructural understanding where a number of connections may be made, but the meta-connections between them are missed, as is their significance for the whole. The origins of each student's household inputs are considered as to whether these are mined, grown or manufactured and how sustainable these are. The students are now able to appreciate the significance of the parts in relation to the whole and are working at the relational level. The students then consider the inputs and outputs of the school, tracking the origin and destination of inputs and outputs. The students are now reaching an extended abstract position where they are making connections not only within the given subject area, but also beyond it, able to generalise and transfer the principles and ideas underlying the specific instance.

There are a range of instructional models based on learning mastery. The key aspects across these approaches are: clearly identified learning goals, regular feedback for students on their progress towards those goals, understanding of metacognitive processes, corrections and advice for students to help them progress, and a learning environment that is conducive to the students being able to meet their goals. Students who believe they can achieve their learning goals (expectancy-value theory), attribute their success to their effort rather than luck (attribution theory), and can see the value of what they are learning (expectancy-value theory) and are supported as and when needed, are most likely to be motivated to focus on learning. Teaching that is focused on students mastering concepts and skills is most likely to be successful, as this is the measure of achievement in the current system.

Mastery of the concept or skill is when the learner has a thorough understanding, they can discuss, explain and demonstrate mastery within the learning context and consider applications beyond the context. To be successful the student must be making connections between the learning tasks and the concepts or skills that they are to master. The students may be fully engaged in a learning task and meet all the set requirements and therefore it could be observed to be very effective teaching from a behaviourist perspective, but without connections between tasks and the concepts or skills students will focus on task goals, and learning, if it occurs, is incidental, dependent on task design and student disposition.

The way the teacher frames their rhetoric can orient students to learning or to task completion. A teacher who talks about completing 'work' is focusing students on the behavioural aspects of learning at school. Alternatively, a teacher who talks about learning progress, weaving the concepts, methods, or skills being mastered into classroom rhetoric, is focusing students on thinking about their learning and making connections. Teacher orientation can be reflected in the expectations of the behaviour within the learning environment, whether it is a place for compliance ('behave in a way that lets the teacher teach') or for learning ('behave in a way that allows yourself and your peers to focus on learning'). Digital age teachers prioritise student learning progress in their rhetoric and as they make pedagogical decisions.

Diversity in learning

There will be diversity in the speed and depth at which learners learn skills and master concepts, which creates complexity in the process of teaching. Teachers are expected to meet the learning needs of all students and all students are expected to achieve curriculum outcomes. This causes tension due to schooling structures and diversity in the student population (Slavin, 1987). The curriculum sets the expectations of student learning.

A curriculum designed with expected outcomes aligned with ages of children may be underpinned with a norm referenced expectation of student achievement. The expectations in such a curriculum may be that students do some learning around each of the stated aims with some reaching mastery level (Figure 8.6).

The creation of knowledge requires mastery of concepts and skills and a further exploration of these, including the mashing together of different concepts. A digital age curriculum may set the minimum level of learning for all students at mastery. A teacher using such a curriculum would plan learning experiences so that those learners who reach a mastery level first will be applying the concepts and skills they have mastered to develop knowledge further. Learning experiences include sufficient assessment opportunities to enable appropriate monitoring of student progress and subsequent teaching to ensure all students reach mastery level. It may be that not all students begin to develop knowledge which provides flexibility within the students' learning experiences (Figure 8.7).

The effective teacher in the digital age teaches in a way that encourages mastery learning and knowledge creation, builds learning relationships, makes teaching decisions based on evidence and guides student learning through targeted formative feedback. Being aware of student learning progress informs the teaching practice.

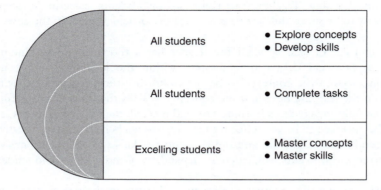

Figure 8.6 Differentiated learning outcomes in teacher centred model of schooling.

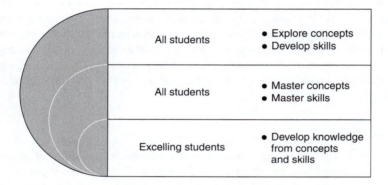

Figure 8.7 Differentiated learning outcomes in learner centred model of schooling.

Evidence based teaching

A teacher in the digital age gathers, analyses, and uses evidence of student learning throughout the teaching process. Student learning is an ongoing process and the teacher who is focused on learning monitors progress to report on learning, responds appropriately, and refines professional practice.

There is a range of evidence of learning that can be used to inform teaching in the digital age. Informal evidence from student 'think alouds', written or verbal responses to questions, and quiz or activity processes and results. Thinking aloud is a process used in educational research to explore the thinking processes explained by Ericsson (2006). A student verbalising what they are thinking as they are learning or carrying out a task can give the teacher valuable insight into their understanding and what to teach at that particular time. This can be a digital attachment to the learning task. The more formal evidence can be downloaded through interactive educational programmes which guide student learning, quizzes, tests and examinations which the students undertake during the learning process along with student directed evidence of learning.

The evidence of learning will align with the concepts, skills, and knowledge creation that form student and teacher negotiated interpretations of the national, regional or local curriculum. The data that is incorporated into the student learning record will need to be robust if it is to be useful. The teacher will be experienced in gathering evidence of learning against curriculum benchmarked concepts, skills and knowledge creation. The student record will reflect ongoing learning progress.

If the students are learning about the concept of entrepreneurship their record of learning will include whether they have learnt the components of the concept such as advertising, original design and profit. It will link to an example of when the student demonstrated understanding of these and whether the student was able to draw these together to explain entrepreneurship in one or more contexts, or ultimately to demonstrate entrepreneurship and explain how the concept is linked to decisions the student made. At the appropriate place in the record of learning notes about how the student understood the concept would be made which may include a link to a sample of student work that demonstrates their learning or progress towards understanding the concept. This may be recorded directly if the record of learning is mashed with educational software.

A digital record of learning will be similar to a medical record. It will belong to the student and be accessible to the student, their family and the school or learning organisation to which they are enrolled. A student's record will include progress against benchmarked curriculum levels, national cohort comparisons, and learning goals which are negotiated between the teacher, the student and the family based on evidence of learning progress.

Attached to each student's record will be links to knowledge created and debated beyond the learning environment. In the digital age exemplars of a student's learning can be collated by the learner who can download a sequence for a specific purpose from his or her record of learning. This idea builds on the notion of a portfolio which emerged in the paper based pre-digital environment.

Analysis

Evidence of learning progress will be analysed and reported to the student, their family, the teacher and the management team at the school. Analysis is done on an individual student basis.

Evidence of student learning will be analysed. It will be evaluated against expected progress which can be plotted based on national data averaged over the years or the individual student's negotiated progress. Individual learning progress results will be discussed with the teacher and the student. The evidence can be used to set future learning goals and inform the individual students' learning programme or feedback being given.

The teacher will analyse the cohort data prior to teaching students to inform the decisions about content, context, and levels of learning activities and expectations of students. The cohort data will be tracked over time to see if the learning progresses at the expected level. They can also check to see how the cohorts progress in one year compared to other years and compared to different teachers. The teacher will analyse data and explain or explore why any results differ from expectations and adjust teaching to maximise learning when appropriate. On some occasions the learning may be occurring in areas that are not being measured, so the evidence base needs to be flexible enough to recognise learning that occurs beyond the specific aspects within a curriculum document.

The school management team will use the evidence to analyse data to set policies and goals for cohort or school wide goals. The student learning records can be collated to compare learning progress within cohorts, comparing groups such as those taught by different teachers, different subjects, cultural or ethnic groups. Student achievement can be compared from one year to another tracking the same cohort to compare how they achieve over time within individual subjects or learning areas.

The teacher can also examine cohort learning data to identify any aspects in which they need to improve, or aspects in which they excel.

Using evidence with students

As the teacher examines student learning they make judgements on what has been learnt and what the student should learn or master next. Research that explores effective feedback on learning has identified a number of features that can help learners.

Clarke (2001) examined how students responded to teachers' written feedback and found that too many criteria made it very difficult for specific feedback to be given and students were overwhelmed when too much information was included. In the digital age student feedback on learning, whether written, verbal, or automated through a programme should be specific to the learning or criteria, be co-constructed and highlight learning achievements, and guide the student to the next aspect to learn and how to learn this.

The content of learner feedback is important. Pat Tunstall and Caroline Gipps (1996) developed a typology of teacher feedback by recording and classifying the feedback given by teachers to students. They classified feedback as either evaluative (involving a value judgment) or descriptive (describing what the student said or did).

Evaluative feedback involves a judgement by the teacher based on implicit or explicit norms. For example: 'That's a good essay' or 'You've done well'. This type of feedback can have a short-term motivational effect on learners, but it is unlikely to help the learner to develop their understanding of concepts, skills or construct knowledge.

Descriptive feedback makes specific reference to the student's learning progress. An example of descriptive feedback would be: 'That's a good advert because you have made connections between the product and the target market and explained your thinking behind your choice of images. Now … which aspects could you animate to maximise the appeal for your target market and how will you know if your advertisement is likely to be successful?' This feedback requires the student to respond to the next learning steps and consider how they will achieve their learning aim.

The teacher who is giving formative feedback on the collaboration and creation of knowledge in the digital age analyses student progress in the virtual or physical learning environment. Effective feedback to the student is focused on the student's learning progress and uses the criteria and language introduced and developed between the teacher and the students. If new language is introduced it is discussed and explained and a common understanding of terminology established.

Quality feedback:

- is focused on learning;
- occurs as the students are learning (timely);
- is descriptive, with specific information;
- is framed within the context of student learning progress;

- is a discussion with co-construction rather than 'telling';
- is strategic to help the student to learn.

The judgements that a teacher makes about student learning and the relevant feedback to be given are a professional response based on their knowledge and training. Samples of these decisions are moderated and discussed through formal and informal teacher networks and difficult decisions can be made collaboratively within the teaching profession. Teacher professional knowledge is created and developed through discussion, research and debate around core decisions about the use of learning evidence.

When a teacher has comprehensive pedagogical content knowledge they are able to help students to learn and construct knowledge more effectively than when their decisions are based on generic pedagogical knowledge. A study of beginning teachers found that strong substantive subject and pedagogical content knowledge enhanced their confidence and ability to be innovative in teaching approaches and responsive to their students' learning (Starkey, 2010). A teacher without substantive knowledge of the subject they are teaching will be limited in the feedback they are able to give their students and may not be aware of their limitations. Without the substantive knowledge of the subject student learning may be limited to either discovery or inquiry type learning which focuses on task completion or students working methodically through a textbook or computer adaptive program. These teaching strategies can give students a basic understanding of a concept or skill, but the teacher will struggle to be responsive to ad hoc student learning needs or extend learning beyond the tasks. The teacher is likely to lack confidence to be innovative or flexible in their teaching approach and unable to give direct teaching or targeted formative feedback to students on their learning about the nuances of the concepts and skills within the subject being taught.

Teachers who are responsive to students through an autonomy-supportive learning environment encourage intrinsic motivation by enhancing student control over their learning progress. Conversely, research by Benware and Deci (1984) found that students who are overly controlled not only lose initiative but also learn less well, especially when learning is complex or requires conceptual, creative processing.

Evaluating teaching occurs at many levels in the digital age. The teacher reflects during the teaching process on how well students are learning and what they can do to help students to learn. At regular times during the year the teacher will evaluate individual and cohort learning against expected progress. Learning will also be evaluated against cohort and school goals or targets.

Teaching in the virtual learning environment

Student cohorts can be more fluid in the digital age. Students from different locations can be grouped together with a teacher or teachers to learn through online learning environments. A teacher may have a special interest learning group, students isolated or at a distance from education or connected for other reasons. The potential for individuals to collaborate through global connections available through digital technology and the Internet enables geographically diverse people to form like-minded groups. Anderson (2006) examined the impact of the Internet on sales and marketing of products which would not be viable in a small geographically bound community. He found that in a global community the market for special interest products such as a particular type of music or book can become profitable and accessible, hence the success of Amazon. He called this phenomenon 'the long tail'. When the long tail is applied to learning rather than the market situation, it means that through the World Wide Web, learners and knowledge creators are able to connect with others in the world with similar interests, to critique and give feedback. The long tail can be applied to school age education, where young people can connect with other learners with similar passions, talents or learning needs.

Teachers with students in a virtual learning environment apply the same teaching principles as those who are teaching their students within the same physical environment. They establish a learning relationship with their students and base their teaching decisions on evidence about the learning needs of the students, the curriculum and the context. They establish goals for each student's learning and monitor their progress, co-constructing, giving feedback and coaching or advising as needed.

Summary

Effective teachers in the digital age context will be part of a highly skilled profession focused on student learning. The teachers will have strong content knowledge appropriate for the level and subjects being taught, pedagogical content knowledge, the ability to cement learning relationships, and understand how to gather, analyse and apply learning data within their teaching practice. Digital innovations provide communication tools, electronic evidence management and analyses systems and will continue to be developed to enable and enhance the process of teaching and learning

The process of teaching will have digital technologies integrated at different levels and stages. The availability of evidence and analysis of student prior learning, current, and anticipated progress is likely to be a revolutionising aspect of the development of the teaching profession. The ability to instantly access annotated evidence and analysis of what and how students have learnt about a concept, principle, method, or skill will help teachers to plan, co-construct and guide student learning experiences. The teaching process will be flexible to be responsive to evidence of student learning progress as they strive to master skills and concepts and create knowledge.

The range of and flexibility of digital learning resources that will be available will enhance the teacher's ability to select appropriate learning experiences that meet the curriculum objectives and identified learning needs of the students that they teach. Understanding how to build effective learning relationships and be culturally responsive will continue to be important features of effective teaching.

The teaching profession will develop through being connected. Professional discussions, which can be facilitated through digital technologies, help share and develop teachers' collective knowledge. Such discussions will focus on priorities for digital age teachers, which include: student learning, conceptual understanding, skill development, knowledge creation and evidence based teaching.

Chapter 9

The start of the digital age

The extent of social changes as a result of digital technological innovations is unknown at the start of the digital age, although the industrial age can provide an indication of the scale that may eventuate. It appears that teaching and learning will evolve over time as people become increasingly connected, technological innovation continues, participation in society is re-examined, and learning theory develops or evolves further. All aspects of society are connected at some level and change in teaching and learning is connected to change in other aspects of education. Change in teaching and learning in the digital age is interwoven with change in national curricular, teachers' work, students' experiences at school, schooling structures and educational policies.

Digital age curriculum

Curriculum in the industrial age was underpinned by a focus on developing a literate and numerate society, with some students being educated further to go into the public sector or to university to study towards professions. How the filtering of students was determined depended on the sociological hierarchical beliefs of the country. Some countries aimed to have the most academically talented students move on to further study by funding their study. Other structures made education available to those from families who could afford to have their children continue in education. Curriculum in senior schools prepared the students for university study.

After the industrial age the school leaving age increased as other skills or knowledge became desirable for all participants in society to draw on. Different tracks emerged within the curriculum for those who were going to work in the trades, be unskilled workers, or manage households and those who were going to continue academic study. Over time this evolved into more fluid curriculum with multiple pathways for students.

The priorities within a school curriculum are a reflection of the society in which it is applied. If the aim of schooling is to prepare students to participate in society as adults, then the curriculum will outline the knowledge and skills that will enable them to achieve this. A progression of concepts and skills will be included in a curriculum along with statements that link learning to the purpose of schooling.

Digital age curriculum will have flexible guidelines that outline a progression of learning developed by leading educational researchers with expertise in subject specific conceptual and skills development. It will be designed in a way that encourages knowledge creation, collaboration, and critique beyond the physical learning environment. An outcomes based curriculum document can be restrictive and may focus on what a student should be able to do or have learnt at a certain age. Attaching ages to the progressions can restrict the speed of student learning. By having the curriculum as progressions this gives flexibility for the students to be learning at a pace that is appropriate to their individual learning needs and be placed in appropriate cohorts. Such a change in curriculum and policy design may see the rate of student learning across the sector increase, which will have implications for the overall knowledge and educational outcomes of schooling within society.

Underpinning a curriculum are the concepts and skills that the students will be learning. These are not discrete learning outcomes, rather they are complexly connected. Eva Baker (2011) and the US National Center for Research on Evaluation, Standards, and Student Testing (CRESST) group have suggested that an ontology based architecture can give a structure to the connections between the aspects of subject knowledge and methods which underpin curriculum. Such an architecture can be applied to an evidence database for student learning and inform the mapping of student learning needs, and therefore teaching focus.

In the digital age students are encouraged to not only master concepts and skills, but also to explore how these can be mashed together, used to create knowledge or to examine alternative perspectives which can be shared and critiqued beyond the immediate physical learning environment. This requires curriculum flexibility as the learning is unpredictable and cannot be explicitly stated as a prescriptive content outcome. The concepts, skills and purposes of learning particular subjects can be explicit but if these are outcomes or the ultimate aim of learning then creativity, flexibility and knowledge creation will be limited.

As creativity, flexibility and knowledge creation are key aspects of participation in society in the digital age a curriculum will encourage these learning activities. All students will be expected to master the concepts and skills in the curriculum document and evidence of their learning progress will be linked within a national database. While concepts and skills are explored in different ways, not all students will create knowledge using each concept or skill they have mastered. The nature of knowledge created will be flexible and unpredictable. This flexibility allows students in a cohort to have divergent learning experiences which can cater for their specific learning needs. Knowledge created by learners will be recorded and linked to their learning record within the national learning database.

Assessment of student progress within the curriculum guidelines may identify whether a student who can describe, explain, or apply a concept to multiple contexts would be considered as achieving formative assessment, as the student who is not yet able to apply the concept to alternative contexts would not have reached a level of mastery and therefore has further learning to complete. Assessment of skills would include whether the student can demonstrate the skill, demonstrate individual expertise in one context or demonstrate the skill in multiple contexts with the latter being at a mastery level. The student who has been able to apply the concept to multiple contexts can explore the boundaries of the concept or skill, consider different perspectives, combine with other concepts or skills, or contemplate 'what if' scenarios. Figure 9.1 is a matrix to illustrate the progression of learning of a concept or skill.

Curriculum is the basis for what is learnt and taught and therefore underpins the awarding of qualifications. If the primary focus of teaching is on learning rather than outcomes or tasks, then this will be reflected in school curriculum and in national or international assessments. Aspects of existing curricular provide an indication of how this flexibility can be incorporated. The Scottish national curriculum contains examples of curriculum statements which can be framed for digital age learners to include the opportunity for the students to

Learning the concept or skill...		Mastery level	Creating knowledge
Description or recognition of the concept	Explain the concept	Apply the concept to multiple contexts	One or more: Explore boundaries of concept or skill Connect with other concepts or skills
Demonstrate the skill	Demonstrate individual expertise in one context	Demonstrate expertise of skill across multiple contexts	Explore alternative perspectives or methods Consider 'what if' scenarios

Figure 9.1 Progression of learning of a concept or skill as a basis for assessment.

create, share and critique their learning through connections (Learning and Teaching Scotland, 2009):

> I can use my knowledge of the interactions and energy flow between plants and animals in ecosystems, food chains and webs. I have contributed [collaboratively] to the design or conservation of a wildlife area.
>
> (SCN 2-02a, p. 260)

> I can discuss [analyse] the sustainability of key natural resources and analyse [discuss] the possible implications for human activity [through a learning network].
>
> (SOC 4-08a, p. 287)

In these examples the [bracketed] additions illustrate how curriculum statements can include knowledge creation through connections.

Entrepreneurship, the circulatory system, poetry, gravity and protest movements are concepts which may be included in a curriculum document. Each concept once mastered can be applied to multiple contexts, such as the circulatory system in different species or during different physical activities, protest movements at different times. Knowledge may be created as the student explores the boundaries of what is poetry, connect together concepts and skills such as entrepreneurship and socialism, explore alternative perspectives of protest movements or consider what if gravity laws were different or the Earth's gravity were altered.

Skills specified in a curriculum document may include formal communication through holographic imaging, physical skills such as basketball shooting, writing, counting or map reading. Each skill can be demonstrated to show individual expertise or mastery by applying the skill to multiple contexts such as shooting basketball hoops from multiple positions on the court, reading different types of maps, using holographic communication in responsive and presentational contexts. Building on the mastery of skills students may be able to create knowledge by exploring the boundaries of basketball shooting through video analysis, mashing skills such as holographic imaging and theatre production, exploring multiple perspectives on writing skills and calligraphy, and considering 'what if' scenarios for counting (for example, what if we had a base 8 system).

The *back to the future* learning activity outlined in Chapter 7 is an example of how participation in society is made explicit across a range of subjects. The students in the original version had expressed an interest in studying what their life would be like in the future. Thus they were examining what their society would be like in the future so that they could consider how they would participate. This activity has a high value placed on learning which enables the teachers to develop challenging tasks knowing that the students are more motivated and will persevere with their learning than if they did not value the learning focus. The learning in this activity is seamless as subjects are integrated.

The careful integration of subjects is logical within a system that is focused on learning and connecting curriculum with participation in society. Curriculum remains important to ensure that across subject domains key concepts and skills are included. It must also be flexible enough to ensure that teachers from those teaching 5-year-olds to those teaching 17-year-olds are able to integrate subjects.

National or regional school curricular should be developed by educational experts who are able to integrate the broad aims of schooling with subject expertise, knowledge of curriculum design and learning theory. The perceived purpose of schooling for the society for which the curriculum is designed should be explicit and underpin the curriculum content. Assuming the purpose is for the next generation of citizens to actively participate in society, the breadth and depth of this aim needs to be explicit to enable understanding by the users of the curriculum. The connection between the curriculum and the teacher's communication with the student is important as it influences the perceived value of the learning by the students which in turn influences motivation and therefore learning progress. If teachers are unable to make the connection between learning and participation in society (in the broadest sense) then the inclusion in the curriculum could be questioned.

A digital age curriculum is developed by educational experts and includes a learning progression of conceptual knowledge, skills and subject methods that once mastered will give students basis to actively participate in the society in which they live. Underpinning the curriculum will be the core values of that society. To actively participate in a digital society citizens interact through digital technology and face-to-face conversations to share, critique and to create knowledge. Such a curriculum needs to have flexibility in its application to allow teachers to tailor learning appropriate for the context, to be able to integrate concepts and skills across subjects and to take students beyond mastery to the creation of knowledge from the concepts and skills being learnt.

Implications for teachers

To teach a digital age curriculum teachers need substantial knowledge and skills. Digital age teachers need a thorough understanding of the concepts, skills and subject methods that they teach, the ability to develop effective physical and virtual learning environments, establish and maintain learning relationships, participating in collaborative and critical professional networks, and to access and maintain an evidence base to inform teaching decisions. Teacher preparation involves university study, specific study in teacher education and mentoring within the teaching context.

Teaching that is focused on learning needs is complex and requires substantial knowledge and expertise. The teacher needs to draw on academic knowledge of the subjects that they are teaching, appropriate pedagogical approaches for the concepts or skills being taught, educational psychology, learner development, and the curriculum. These aspects can be learnt through study at university. The older the students being taught, the greater the academic subject specific knowledge is needed by the teacher. Teachers teaching younger students require substantial academic knowledge about language, literacy, and numeracy development.

Teachers in the digital age need to gather, analyse, and implement decisions based on evidence of student learning needs. This involves understanding learning processes, how to evaluate student learning progress, which data to record, and how to respond to evidence to enhance student learning. The range of knowledge and skills that a teacher develops to teach from an evidence base and with a focus on learning is extensive and learnt through a specific teacher education programme. The digital age teacher will be a member of a highly trained and educated profession.

The digital age teacher has knowledge of a wide range of learning and administration tools. These include digital tools that teachers use for organisation, teaching processes, to enhance student learning and professional learning. Learning how to use digital technologies is integrated within academic study and ongoing professional learning. It is unlikely that learning about digital technologies would be separated from the context or offered as a separate programme.

Building and maintaining learning relationships is an important aspect of teaching and learning in the digital age. Schooling and education involves learning through connections and the relationships that learners have are an important aspect of the learning process. Learning relationships between teachers and their students are initiated and developed by the teacher who is the adult in the relationship. It is the quality interactions about learning between a teacher and a student that form the basis of a learning relationship. To be effective the conversations (virtual or face-to-face) are underpinned by the teacher's substantial knowledge of each learner, the subject, skills, concepts and pedagogy. Learning to build and maintain learning relationships occurs through a teacher education programme and through practical application within the learning context.

A further implication for digital age teachers is the connections they will need to establish and maintain with learners who may not be within the same physical environment as themselves. The principles for teaching students are the same for students who are at a distance to the teacher as those who are physically in the same room. The teacher needs to establish a learning relationship, identify learners' needs from curriculum, the context and evidence, teach, and monitor their progress. To be successful the teacher needs to be able to build a learning relationship through the online environment. This includes: getting to know the students, their learning interests and needs, being responsive, demonstrating they care about the student's learning progress and adjusting the teaching and learning programme based on evidence. The way that this is done varies according to the synchronicity and communication opportunities which exist in the learning environment and the time that the teacher has available.

A science teacher may be allocated a year to teach a cohort of 15-year-old students physics. The students may be situated in four different rural communities. The first weeks of learning will be carefully designed to establish learning relationships, a pattern of learning for the students and learning expectations and targets. The teacher may establish a pattern of learning for the students based on independent and group study, and synchronous tutorials where students are asked questions, ask questions, or present an aspect of their learning for critique. Prior to teaching the students the teacher will examine and consider their progress of learning, particularly in the aspects pertaining to physics. The teacher will access samples of each student's knowledge building from previous years and develop targets and a teaching plan for the cohort. An initial learning activity may involve exploring physics within the student's local context.

The *back to the future* themed learning unit outlined in Chapter 7 was developed for a cohort of students living in different locations across the globe. The students were taught by a team of teachers, each with different subject expertise. One teacher was allocated to be the key mentor for each student and established a strong learning relationship with that student and their family. A feature of this learning unit was the integration of the subjects without losing the integrity of the conceptual knowledge and skills specific to subject domains. It was a complex process of collaboration and planning then guiding students based on the evidence of their learning. Keeping students motivated and focused on the learning process was challenging. It can be difficult to identify when a student is not focused on learning in a physical classroom and being present in class tends to be the default measure. In the online environment logging on can be a default measure, although a better one is the quality of the shared learning and reflections with peers, the teacher and beyond the learning environment which provides evidence of the learning that is occurring.

The connections a teacher has are an important source of advice, support and professional learning. Within a learning environment such as a school, a teacher may have a range of people with whom he or she can discuss and critique their teaching and their students' learning progress. However, they may need to have connections beyond the learning environment for support and learning which targets specific pedagogical content knowledge. A professional network of colleagues with specialist knowledge in the same field is essential for quality conversations that lead to professional learning. For example, a teacher of 5-year-olds can discuss the unique learning and teaching issues faced with learning to read, develop text and count or manipulate numbers. The teacher of physics benefits from conversations, support and advice from other teachers with strong pedagogical content knowledge within physics. Such learning networks can be extensive and include researchers and academics.

Teaching is not an individualistic profession; a healthy education system has strong formal and informal teacher networks through which professional discussions take place. Through these networks learning occurs and is shared across the profession. Teachers collaborate and discuss teaching strategies, curriculum implementation, innovations, student learning progress, knowledge creation, and being a teacher through networks established through the schools, universities, regions or social media. Formal structures within school may require teachers to collaborate to discuss planning, assessment and student learning progress. There may be formal professional learning groups, regional subject or special interest networks and global social networks. Instant communication capabilities enable collaboration and support.

In the digital age formal and informal conversations about student learning progress based on evidence are an important aspect of teaching. Such discussions can be for moderation purposes, collaborative decision making and professional learning. The participants in a discussion about evidence based learning will be developing a shared understanding about whether and when students are adequately demonstrating mastery of a skill or concept, what students' next learning steps should be, or evaluating knowledge creation. Such collaboration is similar to the way that the medical profession collaboratively considers a diagnosis or course of treatment. The broader the participants and the greater the frequency of critical conversations, the greater the learning will be across the profession. Within schools or learning organisations professional conversations form part of professional accountability and learning.

The exploration of learning progress across cohorts of students is a focus of professional conversations within and across learning organisations. Electronic learning records allow the aggregation of data. Synthesised data is analysed to identify patterns which inform policy decisions about groups of students, learning aspects, or teacher practice to be the focus for specific interventions. Outstanding teaching, regional learning differences, or patterns of learning progress of identifiable groups of students can be ascertained through the examination of aggregated student learning progress data. For example, over three years the students taught by teacher X have mastered the concept of gravitational forces quicker and actively created knowledge at a higher quality than other students in the region. This teacher becomes the focus of research which explores his or her teaching strategies, learning relationships, use of evidence for teaching, context, and students' learning experiences to identify possible reasons for success and the findings are shared through the professional networks. Such findings may include multimedia presentation of the teacher outlining their practice which leads to rich discussion through a social media network.

The aggregated student learning progress data may identify a group of students who struggle to master a specific or a range of concepts or skills. This result can be explored through examining variables within the data and further literature and contextual research in the specific identified area of concern. The teachers of the students and educational experts, who may be teacher educators or leading teachers from another learning context, collaboratively develop interventions to accelerate the learning of the group. An evaluation of the process and results are shared and discussed across the professional learning community, thus enhancing the shared knowledge of the network of practitioners.

Teaching in the digital age involves constructive scrutiny of professional judgements. The critical evaluation of teaching decisions underpins the systemic accountability processes in evidence based professional teaching practice. Such scrutiny is through the examination of student learning progress and the evaluation of teaching decisions at the cohort and individual levels. Each student has their anticipated learning progress over time plotted within the electronic learning management system. This is developed using evidence from national data sets and student–teacher–family goal setting discussions. Each teacher will be able to justify the goals that they have set for students, the decisions made, and their judgement on the level of student learning progression. This critical evaluation occurs through a reflective learning conversation based on a range of evidence. There are two aspects to such discussions – the first is the boundaries of judgements, which should be similar across the profession, thus the discussions form part of a moderation process. The second aspect is the detail of decisions and implications for teaching and learning. These discussions would unpack understanding of the concept or skill, evidence of student learning progress and the next learning focus that was identified and shared with the student.

The evidence of learning informs target setting. Using data from across cohorts and years school management teams set goals for learning or knowledge creation achievement on an annual basis or across a number of years. For example, the data may indicate that an identifiable group of students at the learning institution do less well on aspects of the curriculum than other students. Targets and a plan can be formulated after exploring possible reasons and solutions through existing education research, talking to the students, their families, the teachers and experts in the field.

The data may indicate differences in the learning progressions of students being taught by different teachers. Analysis of such data includes comparison of the specific students within a group over their schooling history within specific domains of learning. It could be that the students in different teaching groups have had different learning pathways or consistently progressed to higher or lower levels of learning than their peers. Comparison of student achievement within certain learning areas across the years could indicate that students who are taught by a certain teacher appear to learn less or more than those taught by other teachers. A targeted and comprehensive professional learning programme may improve a teacher's performance when it is identified as less than adequate or, if unsuccessful, a change in career direction may be warranted. A teacher whose students are consistently creating, sharing and critiquing knowledge at a higher level than their peers may be invited to share their expertise through teacher networks and become a mentor or lead teacher.

The digital age has implications for the work, knowledge and skills of teachers. A teacher's job becomes even more complex as they focus on the learning progress of students, multiple learning environments and collegial and critical professional networks. Effective teachers in the digital age have extensive academic knowledge of what they are teaching, how students learn and create knowledge, how to critique and use evidence to inform their teaching practice, and how to establish and maintain learning relationships within their teaching and professional contexts. The practice of teaching is enabled by the use of digital tools and the extensive information and analysis of student learning progress.

Implications for students

Being a student will have some fundamental differences in the digital age when compared to the learning experiences of school students of the past. There will be no need for students to carry books to and from school, which may put the concept of school bags into the history books. They will just need their digital device(s), which are likely to be compact and highly portable, and their sports or extracurricular materials which likewise will have evolved further.

Schooling hours are likely to be aligned with digital age societal functioning rather than an agrarian working calendar. This means that students may be in a learning environment from 8 am to 5 pm, or may have flexible learning hours depending on how work patterns alter in response to the widespread use of digital technologies within the community. It would seem unlikely that summer breaks lasting months and other long breaks through the year would continue in the digital age unless adult working patterns change.

In the digital age learning how to learn collaboratively and being connected with the local community through friendships will remain important skills for a caring and participatory society. Therefore students in the digital age will be attending a learning centre within their local community as the home base of their education. It is through that learning community that friendships and learning relationships will be established. At each level of schooling the student will have a strong learning relationship with at least one teacher. That teacher will monitor their learning progress, establish goals, and regularly discuss progress with the student and their family. The student may also be part of virtual learning communities for certain subjects, topics or projects depending on their learning needs.

As students progress through the schooling system they will be able to sustain greater levels of independent and group learning between intensive feedback from their teachers.

Thus secondary-age students may have flexible learning timetables that are collaboratively scheduled through their electronic calendar. Within their weekly calendar they may have cohort tutorials, group learning activities and independent learning time. An example of how this might look is included in Figure 9.2.

In this example a student may have had the tutorials, presentations, and meetings put into his or her electronic timetable centrally by the teachers planning the learning. The student would add in the learning with peers and preparation for tutorials in conjunction with the teachers and peers. The extracurricular activities may be added by the relevant coach or team organiser.

For each learning activity the student will have access to a teacher and peers through their digital learning device or through discussion with those in close proximity. For tutorials the teacher may be in the same room. Each week the student may have a scheduled personal 15 minute discussion with one of their teachers about their learning progress. The location and availability of teachers and students is easily accessible through their digital devices which can be automatically updated through their timetable and GPS location.

A student in the digital age may belong to a few cohort groups, the range depending on their learning needs and perhaps the passions of the students. Some cohorts may include students from beyond the physical school environment and the teacher of that cohort may be located at a different educational institution. A virtual learning environment provides flexibility with cohorts as they are not constrained by the physical learning space. A student may be part of a core learning group of three students who regularly discuss their learning progress, schedules and metacognitive strategies and offer support to each other.

Students may be learning subjects or topics at different learning institutions through virtual learning environments. All the learning activities in the student's timetable could be with a teacher and students who are not physically at the same school, perhaps with the exception of the hockey practice and games (unless holographic games evolve). This opportunity allows the students to be in cohorts with other students who are at a similar level in their learning or with the same passions or interests. For example, it allows for the matching of a group of 15 highly capable chemists or musicians to learn at an accelerated rate and explore the boundaries of theories and practice collaboratively under the guidance of an expert teacher in the subject. Such learners may or may not be the same age.

The digital age student will monitor their own learning progress and develop an extensive repertoire of metacognitive skills. Rather than being passive receivers of information who then copy and repeat back information, they master concepts and skills then explore how these can be used, applied and developed in different contexts. There is an expectation that all students master key concepts and skills. They will explore these both within their learning context and beyond it through a virtual learning environment. To accomplish this students develop critical and creative thinking skills. The digital technologies enhance their ability to use metacognitive processes, perhaps through prompts or suggested methods that can be used for different types of activities the students are carrying out. Students already have opportunities to share their creativity and access experts beyond the physical learning environment. This is happening at the start of the digital age with the opportunity for music students in New Zealand to develop and record an original composition, with the best 30 as judged by a team of industry experts gaining the opportunity to receive mentoring by an expert in the field and the opportunity to record their composition in a studio before being released to the public. Senior students of art and design are required to present their designs

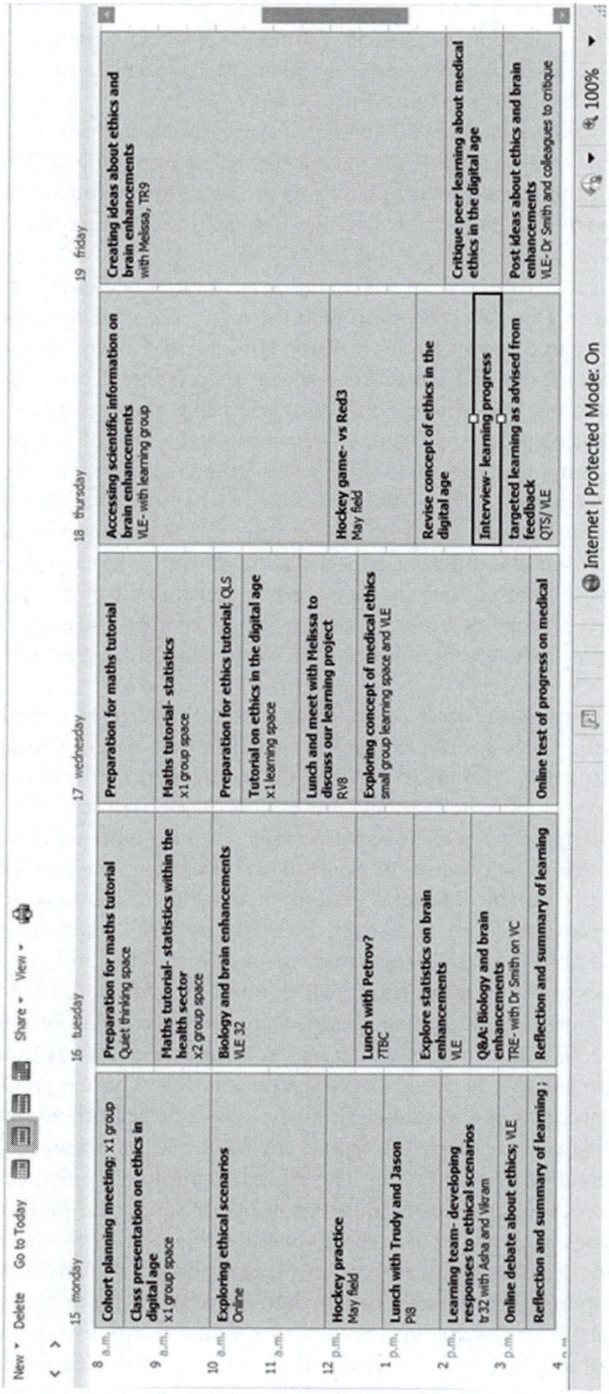

New ▾   Delete   Go to Today   [icons]   Share ▾   View ▾

	15 monday	16 tuesday	17 wednesday	18 thursday	19 friday
8 a.m.	Cohort planning meeting: x1 group	Preparation for maths tutorial Quiet thinking space	Preparation for maths tutorial	Accessing scientific information on brain enhancements VLE- with learning group	Creating ideas about ethics and brain enhancements with Melissa, TR9
9 a.m.	Class presentation on ethics in digital age x1 group space	Maths tutorial- statistics within the health sector x2 group space	Maths tutorial- statistics x1 group space		
10 a.m.	Exploring ethical scenarios Online	Biology and brain enhancements VLE 32	Preparation for ethics tutorial; QLS		
11 a.m.			Tutorial on ethics in the digital age x1 learning space		
12 p.m.	Hockey practice May field	Lunch with Petrov? 7TBC	Lunch and meet with Melissa to discuss our learning project RV8	Hockey game- vs Red3 May field	
1 p.m.	Lunch with Trudy and Jason P18	Explore statistics on brain enhancements VLE	Exploring concept of medical ethics small group learning space and VLE	Revise concept of ethics in the digital age	Critique peer learning about medical ethics in the digital age
2 p.m.	Learning team- developing responses to ethical scenarios tr32 with Asha and Vikram	Q&A: Biology and brain enhancements TRE- with Dr Smith on VC		Interview- learning progress	
3 p.m.	Online debate about ethics; VLE	Reflection and summary of learning	Online test of progress on medical	targeted learning as advised from feedback QTS/VLE	Post ideas about ethics and brain enhancements VLE- Dr Smith and colleagues to critique
4 p.m.	Reflection and summary of learning ;				

Internet | Protected Mode: On   🔍 100%

Figure 9.2 Student timetable.

in a public forum which has resulted in media interest and feedback from clients or experts. These specific links between learning at school and participating in society can enhance motivation and a student's sense of personal identity. These types of specific learning and sharing experiences are likely to increase in the digital age.

Students create ideas by applying concepts and methods to real problems facing their community, nation or the global environment. Problem solving involves collaborative exploration and findings that are shared with those who are in a position to implement the ideas. Students may mash together ideas or concepts to consider different ways of thinking, or explore different perspectives of a concept.

The communication between the teacher and the parents can be instant and seamless in a digital society, which is particularly useful at the secondary school level when teenagers become increasingly independent from their families and parents have few opportunities to pop in and talk with a teacher. Thus the relationship between the teacher and parent is likely to be stronger than when it was reliant on paper notes brought home by the student interspersed with school based meetings, school camps or sporting events.

Students in the digital age may become 'digital natives' once the technology is advanced enough and available so that each person has a portable networked device(s) that becomes an extension of their brain. They will no longer be learning to write using pen and paper; instead they will learn to communicate through text, symbols, orally and other methods relevant to the context and time. The basis of learning will always be the thinking processes carried out by an individual student no matter what technologies become available. The digital devices will be integrated into learning processes enhancing the student's organising, processing, storing and communicating capabilities.

As students explore concepts and skills they will critique their progress, give critical feedback to their peers and seek critique of their ideas from within their learning environment and beyond. Through this process they will be sharing their ideas and contributing to the development of knowledge in a context that is broader than their own learning space. This will enhance the image of the digital age school as a place of knowledge processing.

Implications for schools

Will schools even exist in the digital age? If we assume that people are going to continue to live within community groups with extensive connections beyond their neighbourhood then schools may continue to play an important role within a community. Schools currently serve a social function as a place where neighbourhood children establish friendships and acquaintances which extend beyond the schooling environment (in context and in years). The children play or hang out together after school and at weekends and in doing so informal learning and peer teaching takes place. Their connections through online and community social networks extend beyond their years at school.

Schools commonly serve an important function within a community. The local school provides a place where students learn about events, people and the social history of the community. It is rich with local resources including the people who live and work within the area, the natural and cultural environment and social issues. Using local resources, events and issues can help students to understand the learning they are undertaking and hence it can motivate and enhance learning progress. Through knowing about the community in which they live students incorporate it into their identity enhancing their sense of belonging and identity.

The facilities within a school may be used for community activities such as emergency shelters, evening classes, performances, meetings, sporting competitions, and casual places where neighbourhood young and not so young can meet and play. Schools have an important role as a key feature of society, contributing to the fabric of a community. Although the nature of schools may change in the digital age, the community connection is likely to remain strong.

The original purpose of compulsory schooling was to ensure that education reached the masses so that they could effectively contribute to society by being numerate and literate. Most schools were located in places where students could travel to and from on a daily basis. In the digital age it is likely that governments will continue to desire to have all their citizens educated with a purpose of effective contribution to society of the future. If the focus within such a system is on learning rather than teaching or outcomes then the education is likely to occur through a community based physical location.

As teachers focus on students learning to use concepts and skills to create and share knowledge through a connected learning environment, the function of schools within communities is likely to evolve. Students can share the knowledge they are creating through the school's online learning environment, thus it becomes a place of thinking, creativity and critique. Schools will become producers of knowledge, sharing the learning that is emerging with the wider community. Schools may ultimately become perceived as knowledge centres within communities where learning extends to knowledge creation that is shared beyond the school's physical and virtual boundaries. Figure 9.3 illustrates the connections through which knowledge is developed and shared with the community, other schools and global society.

People are social beings and learning does not occur in isolation. The possibility of computers guiding student learning through immediate feedback and multiple pathways

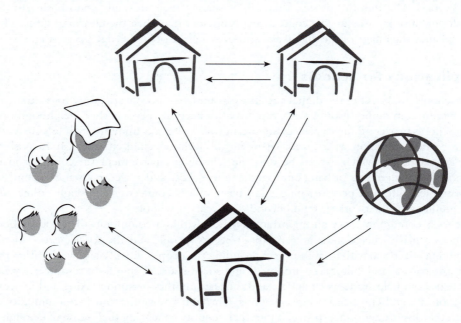

Figure 9.3 Schools developing and sharing knowledge within society.

according to their responses to questions was considered as a possible way of learning at the start of the digital age. Programmes such as computerised adaptive learning have been developed to teach specific concepts and skills and these have become useful learning tools. However, due to motivation, the need for social contact, and to think creatively about concepts and skills, these are likely to remain as tools within a programme which a teacher develops based on student learning needs. In the digital age it is unlikely that the dominant mode of instruction will be through set sequential learning programmes facilitated by teachers.

The relationship between a student and their teacher is an important aspect of learning. A successful education system in the digital age will enable and encourage these relationships to develop. That does not mean for every learning activity, but there must be at least one significant learning relationship with the teacher responsible for the overall progress of the student.

The design of the digital age school will be cognisant of developing the learning relationships between the teachers and the students, a focus on pedagogical approaches for learning concepts and skills and knowledge creation. School based learning in the digital age is unlikely to be primarily viewed as students sitting behind desks or on a mat with the teacher dominating the conversation, although this may occur when it is the best method of instruction for the students' learning needs. In a school which aims to be democratic there will not be different spaces for staff and students. There will be rooms or spaces which have different functions such as different sized meeting rooms, silent thinking spaces, highly creative or interactive spaces with virtual reality functionality for conferencing beyond the school environment or for mastering skills. It is unlikely that pens and paper will be used as they are now and resources for learning will be predominantly digital or people based. Storage space for paperwork and books will not be necessary, but tactile equipment will continue to enhance student learning.

A virtual learning environment in the digital age will eventually have open boundaries and different spaces for the types of learning interactions. The spaces will be flexible to enable students' personal learning environment, external resources, and functionality to be integrated.

Digital devices fit seamlessly into the design. It is unlikely that schools will be immediately rebuilt, it is more likely that existing structures will be adapted through regular upgrades and property development plans.

The school structures are evolving in the digital age. For flexible cohorts across educational centres to be effective the structures, policies and procedures need to be established. Such cross-institution collaborative models could include shared leadership, governance and funding models. Online computer programmes can be used to facilitate and organise or broker the matching process of teachers and students across a region, nation or globally. At the start of the digital age such a process existed within New Zealand for establishing cohorts to learn through the virtual learning network; this was primarily for rural students to access a wider range of senior subjects than their schools were able to offer. The cohorts of students were allocated a teacher and were taught through a virtual learning environment and video-conferencing which was not embedded within the virtual learning environment due to the technological capability of the time.

Flexible timetabling is likely to be a challenge to develop and effectively introduce within and across schools. Educators are likely to value flexible timetabling when they are: focused on their students' learning, using a flexible curriculum, and confident in their subject knowledge, pedagogical content knowledge and use of an evidence base for their teaching decisions.

In summary, schools in the digital age will continue to be situated within communities although the facilities and structures are likely to evolve. The function of schools may be repositioned as a place for the development and sharing of knowledge in the community.

Implications for the national or state policy makers

Education policies are an integral component of the schooling structures and practices. Policies are influenced by government priorities, available funding, international and local trends and, in some contexts, lobby groups.

The idea that all students must have learnt a skill or concept by a certain age is understandable within an industrial age context where diversity enhanced the ability of the schooling system to sort students into professional, labouring or domestic pathways by 10 years of age. This idea does not fit within a society where students are encouraged to stay in formal learning through to 20 years of age.

Two types of accountability models, external and internal, were conceptualised in an OECD literature review (Rosenkvist, 2010). External accountability, also known as bureaucratic or hierarchical, is centrally led with the purpose of measuring the performance of the public schooling sector which is government funded. The accountability is underpinned by the school being a policy instrument with performance measured at the national, regional and local level through student academic achievement. The accountability may be through meeting standards, targets, or goals at an individual teacher, school, regional or national level and may involve incentives and consequences. The external model in OECD countries since the 1990s has led to a culture of hyper-accountability, where schools or teachers are blamed for a range of shortcomings in society or the education system.

A second type of accountability model is the internal or professional accountability model which is underpinned by the belief that teachers are the experts in the complex process of schooling, with skills and knowledge of teaching and learning within their context. The teachers are held accountable for their professional behaviour, measured against standards set by a professional body or government and monitored by peers. The assessment of student learning was not included in this form of accountability. These two types of accountability models can be considered at the extreme ends of a pendulum, with professional accountability more common prior to 1990 in OECD countries (Figure 9.4).

In the digital age a third type of accountability may be an evidenced based internal accountability which includes teachers being held accountable for their students' learning. This model fits between the hyper-accountability and professional models (Figure 9.5). Under this third model evidence of student learning is not limited to external centrally organised examinations. Such a movement in accountability models is logical as digital learning records for students and professional conversations about learning progress evolve to become a central component in the process of teaching and learning. Electronic records of learning can be designed to link evidence of demonstrated competency of concepts or skills, creativity, knowledge creation and sharing of knowledge beyond the learning environment. The databases could form the basis of internal and external accountability.

In the digital age there will be national data systems in place for tracking individual and cohort student learning progress. National or state policy makers will be able to analyse

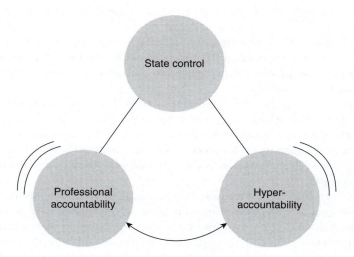

Figure 9.4 Pendulum of state accountability of schooling outcomes.

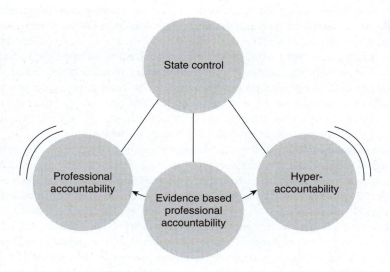

Figure 9.5 Pendulum balance to evidence based professional accountability.

regional, state and national learning progress data to inform support, funding, or policy adjustment decisions. For example, the data set may indicate regional or school differences in rates of scientific conceptual understanding progress between age 8 and 12. Such a discovery would warrant research into those differences and then policy strategies may be appropriate to raise learning progress. This is not to say that all students will be at a certain level, but it would be expected that there is learning progress. Local or regional differences in level may be found by the research to be a result of an agglomeration of scientific industries in one area. Such a community may have greater access to, and priority placed on, scientific knowledge.

The regional data may indicate that at ages 6 to 9 in one area literacy progress slows and this appears to impact on learning across a range of subjects from ages 8 to 11. In this case research, professional support and funding can be directed to the region to improve learning in a way that is relevant to the context.

The evidence based accountability model could include external examination in some form through the use of digital technologies, but consideration would need to be given to what is being tested, whether it is the level of conceptual or skills mastery or whether the creation of knowledge can be measured in such a process. National assessment policies align with purpose and learning theory. If such a system is able to establish a robust evidence base then exams may not be necessary.

The level of conceptual knowledge can be measured through computerised adaptive testing, where students answer questions and their response determines the following test item. Such assessments have been developed for formative evaluation of learners in the areas of mathematics and languages which tend to be sequential in the learning and suited to this form of testing. The use of observation, discussion and student reflection may be a relevant way to explore students' creation of knowledge and interactions through the process of exploring the boundaries and potential of concepts or skills.

External exams prior to the digital age focused on measuring student knowledge and skills against set criteria or outcomes. The examination process failed to evolve at the same rate as teaching and learning processes. During the learning sequences prior to exams the students may have written essays using word processing software and developed their ideas about the concepts and skills being taught. A paper based exam requires quite different metacognitive processes than using word processing software. An essay needs to be developed sequentially and carefully planned before beginning. It is not easy to restructure once begun and deletions and additions require more than a simple cut or paste. It is also not easy to physically write for three hours without extensive experience of penmanship.

The nature of external accountability underpinned the continuation of paper based exams at the start of the digital age as students were increasingly using digital technologies for their learning. A direct change from paper based to digital exams with a similar focus was not immediately feasible. It would not have been possible to have every student with access to fully functioning digital devices needed to complete an exam synchronously located at supervised exam centres given that the students would need to also be familiar with the use of the specific device. Students would not be trusted, or expected, to use digital technologies without communicating with others or accessing information that would help them within the exam. Given that assessment was focused on measuring whether the prescribed knowledge or skills had been learnt, such access may be blocked, but such innovations add to the financial outlay and complexity of exams, making the use of digital devices more expensive than pen and paper.

As digital learning devices become accessible items for each student, externally set exams could be designed that make use of the affordances of digital devices in a controlled synchronous way. For example, a social studies exam that explores student knowledge of the concepts of leadership and conflict in an urban environment may include a range of resources that students access including a homepage with links to information about a scenario including video, statistics, profiles, and history. There may be a simulation activity where students make decisions as a community leader which requires them to apply their conceptual knowledge and explain the reasons behind their decisions, drawing on their understanding of how societies operate and respond to leadership decisions which could include examples of such decisions in the past and different types of community control structures. The exam assessors would receive a summary of decisions made and justifications/explanations that they would use to ascertain a level of mastery of the conceptual knowledge. Assessors base their judgements using assessment rubrics developed through moderation discussions. This type of assessment would not explore knowledge creation.

An examination may have a series of online problems that explore the extent of student understanding of a mathematical concept. How the student answers a problem dictates the following problem that is presented to the student until the level of conceptual understanding is ascertained. Problems could include short video clips such as someone running up an escalator and the student is to find the algebraic equation. Formulating an algebraic equation of distance covered or differentiating to find speed travelled. The programme will ascertain the level of understanding and thus the result of the examination. Mathematics educationalists determine the pathways and levels and the results are added to a student's record of learning.

Figure 9.6 outlines the types of assessment tasks that could be applied through digital technologies, aligned with the different aims of learning. A focus on developing

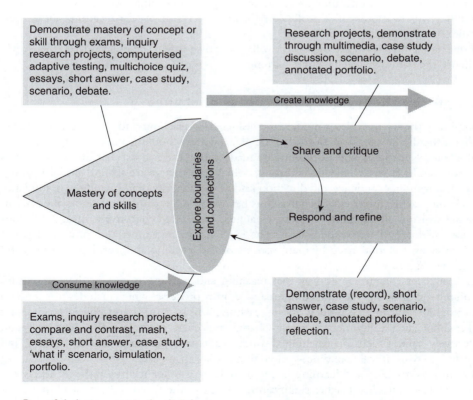

Figure 9.6 Assessment in the digital age.

understanding of prescribed content knowledge can be assessed through exams, inquiry based research projects, and computerised adaptive testing which could include a range of test items. This type of assessment has been the focus since the industrial age. Assessment of students' learning as they explore the concepts and skills that they have mastered can also occur through an examination process, although this would limit collaboration opportunities and the opportunity to receive critical feedback from beyond the learning environment. As students create knowledge assessment is through the students sharing of the knowledge that they develop, such as through an annotated portfolio that illustrates the process and outcomes of their learning. Such assessment is difficult to be included within an examination process. The results of assessments inform the teaching and can be included in the student's electronic record of learning.

Effective assessment which informed learning was identified by Black and Wiliam (1998) as including effective communication between the teacher and the student, a focus on learning rather than grades and having students involved in the learning process. An evidence based accountability model builds on these ideas of effective assessment.

Teachers' work in the digital age will be highly complex requiring in-depth substantive subject knowledge, pedagogical content knowledge, the ability to monitor and assess student learning progress and to gather, analyse and apply evidence of learning. The skill and knowledge required for such a practitioner would place this as one of the most, if not the most, important and complex jobs. As such it should have high or highest status of any profession and remuneration and academic preparation to align with this status. Policies can influence the status of a profession through recruitment, certification, allowances, conditions of work and remuneration.

Educational policies in the digital age will evolve over time. The policies that emerge will influence the nature of teaching and learning.

Complexity theory and the process of change

Complexity theory provides a model to consider how teaching and learning may change through the digital age. Complexity can be identified in schooling and teaching systems at multiple levels through which decisions are made within the context that they exist. Across and between levels are connections through which experiences are shared and ideas developed. Innovation, experience and direction lead to the diversity of ideas and the redundancy of existing practice, policies or beliefs. Thus new knowledge within and across the systems emerges which is unique to the context. Change is moderated collectively through the connections within and across the system. The exact nature and timeframe of change is not predictable as it is influenced by many aspects of the teaching and learning processes and structures (Figure 9.7).

A significant change in the way that teaching and learning occurs in the compulsory schooling sector occurs through complex and lengthy processes which includes teachers and educators altering mental models about teaching, and structures and policies supporting and enabling such realignment to occur. Changing teachers' mental models individually and collectively from a focus on teaching through students completing tasks to learning and knowledge creation will take time – generations rather than years.

Change to teaching and learning in the digital age is influenced by different levels and contexts. The individual teacher significantly influences the focus and extent of his or her students' learning. A teacher's beliefs about learning, pedagogical approaches, and teaching

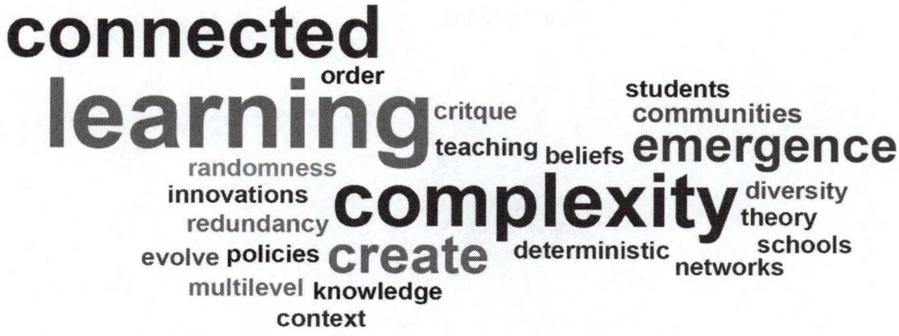

connected
learning order
critque
randomness teaching beliefs
innovations **complexity**
redundancy
evolve policies **create** deterministic
multilevel knowledge
context

students
communities
emergence
diversity
theory
schools
networks

Figure 9.7 Complexity of schooling.

priorities are influenced by his or her experiences and values as well as the context in which they are teaching, including the ideas and innovations they are exposed to through connections with colleagues, peers, media and society in general. Collectively teachers form communities of practice where ideas and experiences develop and are discussed and common understanding established. It is through these formal and informal networks that knowledge emerges.

At all levels of the education sector ideas emerge, with some becoming embedded into the beliefs and practices across the sector and most becoming redundant, refined or replaced. It is through this process of diversity and redundancy of ideas that knowledge within the sector evolves. This is not a democratic process as ideas from some participants carry a stronger influence than others. However, an idea or policy that does not align with current mental models may be resisted across the levels and become redundant, or may change teacher practice in unexpected ways. The introduction of national testing of student performance for accountability purposes to a teacher collective which has focused on teaching rather than student learning may respond by teaching exam techniques and answers to anticipated tasks in the testing regime. Teachers whose focus is on mastering concepts and creating knowledge may consider how students can learn and master the necessary knowledge, explore the boundaries of the concepts and skills and apply these in different contexts and combinations. The exact response to a change is not predictable as it is influenced by context and communication through connections.

Other levels that influence change within a complex education system include the school leaders and the makers of policy who aim to control or guide practice through funding and legislation. Policy decisions are influenced by political process, mandates, government mental models, national and international trends, context and the experiences and connections of those involved.

Complexity theory suggests that emergent knowledge, a new way of thinking about or understanding something, develops at the edge of chaos. The conditions for emergent knowledge have been identified within a classroom context on the *edge* of chaos, where students had a sense of agency and the learning environment was loosely bound (Sullivan, 2009). This compared to a classroom with a tightly bound learning environment where the edge of chaos was avoided and there was minimal student agency. In this latter context emergent knowledge was undetectable.

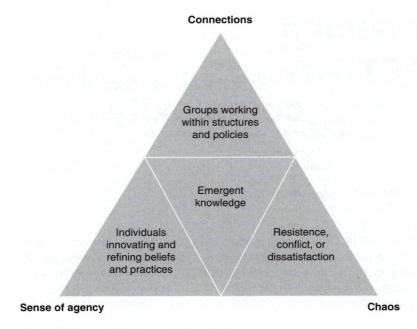

Figure 9.8 Conditions of emergent knowledge.

Knowledge emerges within a system such as the compulsory schooling sector when the participants have a sense of agency, there are connections within and beyond the context, and the system is on the edge of chaos rather than tightly ordered or controlled. Where a balance exists between these conditions emergent knowledge may be stimulated (Figure 9.8). If there is a strong sense of agency amongst individuals or groups within a system (such as teachers or policy makers), minimal connections and a lack of chaos, the individuals or groups may develop knowledge within the confines of their own context and there would be limited impetus or method of discussing or transferring those innovations beyond that context. Being on the edge of chaos without agentic ability to make a change is likely to result in those involved becoming resistant, be in a conflict situation or at the very least dissatisfied with their situation. Strong connections allow for the sharing of ideas and experiences within existing structures and policies, but are unlikely to develop new knowledge without the sense of need from being on the edge of chaos or the perceived authority to do so from a sense of agency. The existence of the edge of chaos can inspire those involved to consider how the situation may be altered, and if the individuals and groups believe they have the power to influence change and are able to share and discuss their ideas through connections, then the condition exists for emergent knowledge.

Complexity theory provides a framework to consider how knowledge might emerge within and across systems in the digital age.

Summary

Compulsory education for children and young adults in the digital age is likely to continue with the underlying aim of maximising participation and advancement of society by the citizens of the future. These are the sentiments that were expressed by Dewey in 1916 and while the detail may be different, the idea remains relevant at the start of the digital age. A national curriculum reflects the priorities of knowledge and skills that are to be learnt by students within the schooling sector and in the digital age these include mastering concepts and skills, being critical, collaborative, and creating knowledge. A digital age curriculum is underpinned by an ontological architectural framework which connects concepts and skills within and across subjects.

Teachers apply the curriculum as they access, gather and analyse data on student learning to inform their teaching decisions. A teacher in the digital age has substantial knowledge and skills and is able to develop and maintain effective learning relationships with their students. They are members of a skilled and highly educated profession and it is through connections or networks across the profession that discussion and critique occurs about student learning progress and teaching practice.

Digital age students may belong to multiple cohorts or learning groups. They are actively involved in the process of learning, guided and supported by their teacher and peers as they master skills and concepts, critique, and create knowledge. Rather than being consumers of knowledge, students are taught to be critical thinkers and creators of knowledge. The students have a sense of agency within the learning process and are focused on their learning and the creation and sharing of knowledge. This requires flexible structures, teaching that is focused on learner progress, and the reframing of schools as community centres of knowledge development within their physical and virtual communities.

Educational policies in the digital age will recognise the long-term positive impact on society of a highly skilled, educated and valued teaching profession. Such policies may include the development of an evidence based professional model for accountability, flexible structures and recruitment and retention incentives which heighten the status of the teaching profession.

Knowledge about teaching and learning will continue to emerge in the digital age. Complexity theory provides a framework for considering how knowledge emerges and evolves within education systems. The conditions for emergent knowledge occur when there are strong connections, a sense of agency and a degree of chaos. It involves the introduction of new and diverse ideas, resources, processes, events or practices, and the redundancy or modification of some existing beliefs, policies or practices. It is through this process of diversity and redundancy, controlled collectively through the connected parts of the system (influenced by historical experiences), that new knowledge emerges which will be unique in some way to the complex system or context.

The digital age promises to issue challenges and rewards for the schooling sector. The ideas contained in this book are projections based on theory and understanding of teaching and learning at the start of the digital age. The development of brain enhancements as outlined in science fiction (for example, Vinge, 1986) have not been considered as they would considerably change the way that people participate and contribute to society.

Notes

5 Creating knowledge

1 This type of activity was observed at Raroa Normal Intermediate School, Wellington, New Zealand.
2 http://scratch.mit.edu/

7 Learning in the digital age

1 The programme was Connect.ed, which began in 2003 through The Correspondence School, New Zealand.

References

Anderson, A. K., Wais, P. E. and Gabrieli, J. D. E. (2006). Emotion enhances remembrance of neutral events past. *Proceedings of the National Academy of Sciences of the United States of America*, *103*(5), 1599–1604. doi: 10.1073/pnas.0506308103.

Anderson, C. (2006). *The long tail*. London: Random House.

Anderson, H. H. (1959). *Creativity and its cultivation*. New York: Harper and Brothers.

Anderson, L. W. and Krathwohl, D. R. (eds). (2000). *A taxonomy for learning, teaching, and assessing: a revision of Bloom's taxonomy of educational objectives*. New York: Longman.

Atkinson, J. W. and Raynor, J. O. (1974). *Motivation and achievement*. Washington, DC: V. H. Winston.

Baker, E. (2011). Assessment in a changing world. Keynote presentation, *Symposium on Assessment and Learner Outcomes*, Victoria University of Wellington, September 2011.

Barrell, J. (2010). Problem-based learning: the foundation for 21st century skills. In J. Bellanca and R. Brandt (eds), *21st century skills: rethinking how students learn* (pp. 175–199). Bloomington: Solution Tree Press.

Becta. (2007). *Harnessing technology review 2007: progress and impact of technology in education*. Coventry: Becta.

Benware, C. A. and Deci, E. L. (1984). quality of learning with an active versus passive motivational set. *American Educational Research Journal*, *21*(4), 755–765. doi: 10.3102/00028312021004755.

Bereiter, C. (2002). *Education and mind in the knowledge age*. Mahwah, NJ: Lawrence Erlbaum.

Berndt, T. J. (2004). Children's friendships: shifts over a half-century in perspectives on their development and their effects. *Merrill-Palmer Quarterly*, *50*, 206–223.

Biggs, J. and Collis, K. (1982). *Evaluating the quality of learning: the SOLO taxonomy*. New York: Academic Press.

Bishop, R. and Berryman, M. (2006). *Culture speaks: cultural relationships and classroom learning*. Wellington: Huia Publishing.

Bishop, R., and Glynn, T. (1999). *Culture counts: changing power relations in education*. Palmerton North: Dunmore Press.

Black, P. and Wiliam, D. (1998). Inside the black box: raising standards through classroom assessment. *Phi Delta Kappan*, *80*(2), 139–148.

Bloom, B. S., Engelhart, M. D., Furst, E. J., Hill, W. H. and Krathwohl, D. R. (1956). *Taxonomy of educational objectives: the classification of educational goals; handbook I: cognitive domain*. New York: Longmans.

Borko, H. and Putman, R. T. (1996). Learning to teach. In D. Berliner and R. Calfee (eds), *Handbook of educational psychology* (pp. 673–708). New York: Simon & Schuster/Macmillan.

Brewer, S. (2006). *Self-influences and foreign language learning: towards an agentic theory*. Retrieved 30 September 2010 from www.self.ox.ac.nz/Conferences/2006.

Brown, M. (2004). *The study of wired schools: a study of Internet-using teachers*. Doctor of Philosophy, Massey University, Palmerston North.

Bryson, B. (2010). *At home: a short history of private life*. London: Doubleday.

Buchanan, M. (2000). *Ubiquity: why catastrophes happen*. New York: Three Rivers Press.

Buhs, E. S., Ladd, G. W. and Herald, S. W. (2001). Peer exclusion and victimization: processes that mediate the relation between peer group rejection and children's classroom engagement and achievement? *Developmental Psychology*, *37*(4), 550–560.

Butler, R. (1999). Information seeking and achievement motivation in middle childhood and adolescence: The role of conceptions of ability. *Developmental Psychology*, *35*(1), 146–163. doi: 10.1037/0012-1649.35.1.146.

Chamot, A. (2004). Issues in language learning strategy research and teaching. *Electronic Journal of Foreign Language Teaching*, *1*(1), 14–26.

Chen, C. H. (2008). Why do teachers not practice what they believe regarding technology integration? *The Journal of Educational Research*, *102*(1), 65–75.

Chui, G. (2000). 'Unified theory' is getting closer, Hawking predicts, *San Jose Mercury News* 23 January, p. 29. Retrieved from www.mercurynews.com.

Cilliers, P. (1998). *Complexity and postmodernism: understanding complex systems*. London: Routledge.

Clarke, S. (2001) *Unlocking formative assessment: practical strategies for enhancing pupils' learning in the primary classroom*. London: Hodder & Stoughton.

Clifford, P., Friesen, S. and Lock, J. (2005). Coming to teaching in the 21st century: study conducted by the Galileo Network. Retrieved 7 November 2005, from http://www.galileo.org/research/publications/ctt.pdf.

Connell, W. F. (1980). *A history of education in the twentieth century world*. Canberra: Curriculum Development Centre.

Cornelius-White, J. (2007). Learner-centered teacher–student relationships are effective: a meta-analysis. *Review of Educational Research*, *77*(1), 113–143. doi: 10.3102/003465430298563.

Cowie, B., Jones, A., Harlow, A., McGee, C., Cooper, B., Forret, M., *et al.* (2008). *Tela: laptops for teachers evaluation: final report years 9–13*. Wellington: Ministry of Education.

Cox, M., Webb, M., Abbott, C., Blakeley, B., Beauchamp, T. and Rhodes, V. (2004). *ICT and pedagogy: A review of the research literature*. London: Department for Education and Skills.

Cuban, L. (2001). *Oversold and underused: computers in the classroom*. Cambridge, MA: Harvard University Press.

Cuban, L., Kirkpatrick, H. and Peck, C. (2001). High access and low use of technologies in high school classrooms: explaining an apparent paradox. *American Educational Research Journal*, *38*(4), 813–834.

Davis, B., and Sumara, D. J. (2006). *Complexity and education: inquiries into learning, teaching and research*. Mahwah, NJ: Lawrence Erlbaum Associates.

De Bono, E. (1985). *Six thinking hats*. Boston: Little, Brown and Company.

Dewey, J. (1900). *The school and society*. Chicago: University of Chicago Press.

Dewey, J. (1916). *Democracy and education: an introduction to the philosophy of education*. New York: Macmillan.

Eisenberg, M. B and Berkowitz, R. E. (1990). *Information problem solving: the Big Six approach to library and information skills instruction*. Norwood, NJ: Ablex.

Eisenberg, M.B., Berkowitz, R.E., Jansen, B.A. and Little, T.J. (1999). *Teaching information and technology skills: the Big6 in elementary schools*. Ohio: Linworth Publishing.

Ennis, R. H. (1962). A concept of critical thinking. *Harvard Educational Review*, *32*(1), 81–111.

Ennis, R. H. (1987). A taxonomy of critical thinking dispositions and abilities. Teaching thinking skills: theory and practice. In J. B. Baron and R. J. Sternberg (eds), *Teaching thinking skills: theory and practice* (pp. 9–26). New York: WH Freeman.

Ennis, R. H. (1989). Critical thinking and subject specificity: clarification and needed research. *Educational Researcher*, *18*(3), 4–10. doi: 10.3102/0013189x018003004.

Ericsson, K. A. (2006). Protocol analysis and expert thought: concurrent verbalizations of thinking during experts' performance on representative tasks. In K. A. Ericsson, N. Charness, P. J. Feltovich and R. R. Hoffman (eds), *The Cambridge handbook of expertise and expert performance*. (pp. 223–241). New York: Cambridge University Press.

Facione, P. A. (1990). Critical thinking: a statment of expert consensus for purposes of educational assessment and instruction. Research findings and recommendations. Newark: American Philosophical Association.

Gawith, G. (1988). *Action learning: student guide to research and information skills*. Auckland: Longman Paul.

Gilbert, J. (2005). *Catching the knowledge wave? The knowledge society and the future of education*. Wellington: NZCER Press.

Gonzalez, C. (2004). The role of blended learning in the world of technology. Retrieved 30 March 2006 from http://www.unt.edu/benchmarks/archives/2004/september04/eis.htm.

Green, H. and Hannon, C. (2007). *Their space: education for a digital generation*. London: Demos.

Green, K. C. (1999). When wishes come true: colleges and the convergence of access, lifelong learning, and technnnology. *The Magazine of Higher Learning*, 31(2), 10–15. doi: 10.1080/00091389909602674.

Halpern, D. F. (1998). Teaching critical thinking for transfer across domains: disposition, skills, structure training, and metacognitive monitoring. *American Psychologist*, *53*(4), 449–455. doi: 10.1037/0003-066X.53.4.449.

Hattie, J. (2009). *Visible learning: a synthesis of over 800 meta-analyses relating to achievement*. Oxford: Routledge.

Hogg, L. (2010). Funds of knowledge: an investigation of coherence within the literature. *Teaching and Teacher Education*, *27*(3), 666–677

Johnson, D. W. and Johnson, R. T. (2010). Cooperative learning and conflict resolution: essential 21st century skills. In J. Bellanca and R. Brandt (eds), *21st century skills: rethinking how students learn* (pp. 201–220). Bloomington: Solution Tree Press.

Johnson, D. W., Johnson, R. T. and Stanne, M. B. (2000). Cooperative learning methods: a meta-analysis. Retrieved 5 May 2011 from http://www.tablelearning.com/uploads/File/EXHIBIT-B.pdf.

Kaplan, A., Gheen, M. and Midgley, C. (2010). Classroom goal structure and student disruptive behaviour. *Educational Psychology*, *72*(2), 191–211. doi: 10.1348/000709902158847.

Kennedy, G. E., Judd, T. S., Churchward, A., Gray, K. and Krause, K.-L. (2008). First year students' experiences with technology: are they really digital natives? *Australasian Journal of Educational Technology*, *24*(1), 108–122.

Kirkpatrick, D. (1994). *Evaluating training programs*. San Francisco: Berrett-Koehler Publishers.

Learning and Teaching Scotland. (2009). *Curriculum for excellence: experiences and outcomes*. Edinburgh: Education Scotland. Retrieved 15 April 2011 from http://www.ltscotland.org.uk/Images/all_experiences_outcomes_tcm4-539562.pdf.

Lenhart, A. and Madden, M. (2005). *Teen content creators and consumers: more than half of online teens have created content for the internet; and most teen downloaders think that getting free music files is easy to do*. Washington, DC: Pew Internet and American Life Project.

Lenhart, A., Madden, M., Macgill, A. R. and Smith, A. (2007). *Teen content creators*. Washington, DC: Pew Internet & American Life Project.

Ling, R. and Yttri, B. (2002). Hyper-coordination via mobile phones in Norway. In J. E. Katz and M. Aakhus (eds), *Perpetual contact: mobile communication, private talk, public performance*. Cambridge: Cambridge University Press.

Macgill, A. R. (2007). *Parents, teens and technology.* Washington, DC: Pew Internet and American Life Project

Marzano, R. J. (2000). *A new era of school reform: going where the research takes us.* Aurora, CO: Mid-Continent Research for Education and Learning.

McDermid, J. (2006). Gender, national identity and the Royal (Argyll) Commission of Inquiry into Scottish Education (1864–1867). *Journal of Educational Administration and History, 38*(3), 249–262.

Ministry of Education. (2007). *The New Zealand Curriculum.* Learning Media.

Ministry of Education. (2008). *Ka hikitia – managing for success: the Maori education strategy 2008–2012.* Learning media. Retrieved 24 August 2009 from http://kahikitia.minedu.govt.nz/.

Mishra, P. and Koehler, M. J. (2008). *Introducing technological pedagogical content knowledge.* Paper presented at the AERA annual meeting, New York.

Morrison, K. (2002). *School leadership and complexity theory.* London and New York: Routledge Falmer.

Moss, G., Jewitt, C., Levacic, R., Armstrong, V., Cardini, A. and Castle, F. (2002). *The interactive whiteboards, pedagogy and pupil performance evaluation: an evaluation of the Schools Whiteboard Expansion (SWE).* London: DfES.

NACCCE (National Advisory Committee on Creative and Cultural Education) (1999). All our futures: creativity, culture and education. Retrieved 17 August 2007 from http://www.dfes.gov.uk/naccce/index1.shtml.

Ng, E. and Bereiter, C. (1991). Three levels of goal orientation in learning. *Journal of the Learning Sciences, 1*(3/4), 243–271.

Nuthall, G. A. (2007). *The hidden lives of learners.* Wellington: New Zealand Council for Educational Research.

Ofsted (2005). Embedding ICT in schools: a dual evaluation exercise. Retrieved 14 April 2007 from http://www.ofsted.gov.uk/Ofsted-home/Publications-and-research/Education/Curriculum/Information-and-communication-technology/Secondary/Embedding-ICT-in-schools-a-dual-evaluation-exercise.

Oppenheimer, T. (1997). The computer delusion. *The Atlantic Monthly, 280*(1), 45–62.

Papert, S. and Harel, I. (1991). Situating constructionism. In S. Papert and I. Harel (eds), *Constructionism* (pp. 1–11). Westport, CT: Ablex Publishing.

Passey, D., Rogers, C., Machell, J. and McHugh, G. (2004). *The motivational effect of ICT on pupils.* Lancaster: Department of Educational Research, Lancaster University.

Pedretti, E., Mayer-Smith, J. and Woodrow, J. (1998). Technology, text, and talk: students' perspectives on teaching and learning in a technology-enhanced secondary science classroom. *Science Education, 82*(5), 569–589.

Piaget, J. (1952). *The origins of intelligence in children* (M. Cook, Trans., 2nd ed.). New York: W W Norton & Co.

Richter-Levin, G. and Akirav, I. (2003). Emotional tagging of memory formation: in the search for neural mechanisms. *Brain Research Reviews, 43*(3), 247–256.

Robinson, V., Hohepa, M. and Lloyd, C. (2009). School leadership and student outcomes: identifying what works and why. *Best evidence synthesis.* Wellington: Ministry of Education.

Rohrbeck, C. A., Ginsburg-Block, M. D., Fantuzzo, J. W. and Miller, T. R. (2003). Peer-assisted learning interventions with elementary school students: a meta-analytic review. *Journal of Educational Psychology, 95*(2), 240–257.

Roschelle, J. M., Pea, R., Hoadley, C. M., Gordin, D. N. and Means, B. M. (2000). Changing how and what children learn in school with computer-based technologies. *The Future of Children, 10*(2), 76–101.

Rosenkvist, M. (2010). *Using student test results for accountability and improvement: a literature review.* Paris: OECD Education Working Papers. doi: 2200559291.

Rowlands, I., Nicholas, D., Huntington, P., Gunter, B., Withey, R., Dobrowolski, T., *et al.* (2008). Information behaviour of the researcher of the future. Retrieved 21 May 2011 from http://www.jisc.ac.uk/whatwedo/programmes/resourcediscovery/googlegen.aspx.

Ryan, R. M. and Deci, E. L. (2000). Intrinsic and extrinsic motivations: classic definitions and new directions. *Contemporary Educational Psychology, 25*, 54–67.

Scardamalia, M. and Bereiter, C. (2006). Knowledge building: theory, pedagogy, and technology. In R. K. Sawyer (ed.), *The Cambridge handbook of the learning sciences.* New York: Cambridge University Press.

Scotland, J. (1969). *The history of Scottish education* (Vol. 1). Edinburgh: University of London Press.

Senge, P., Cambron-McCabe, N., Lucas, T., Smith, B., Dutton, J. and Kleiner, A. (2000). *Schools that learn: a fifth discipline fieldbook for educators, parents, and everyone who cares about education.* New York: Doubleday.

Sheehan, M. (2010). The place of 'New Zealand' in the New Zealand history curriculum. *Journal of Curriculum Studies, 42*(5), 671–691

Shulman, L. S. (1986). Those who understand: knowledge growth in teaching. *Educational Researcher, 15*(2), 4–14.

Shulman, L. S. (1987). Knowledge and teaching: foundations of the new reform. *Harvard Educational Review, 57*(1), 1–22.

Shulman, L. S. and Keislar, E. R. (eds). (1966). *Learning by discovery: a critical appraisal.* Chicago: Rand McNally.

Siemens, G. (2004). Connectivism: a learning theory for the digital age. Retrieved 15 March 2006, from http://www.elearnspace.org/Articles/connectivism.htm.

Siemens, G. (2006). Knowing knowledge. Retrieved 18 November 2006 from http://ltc.umanitoba.ca/KnowingKnowledge/index.php/Main_Page.

Slavin, R. E. (1987). Mastery learning reconsidered. *Review of Educational Research, 57*(2), 175–213.

Stacey, R. D. (2001). *Complex responsive processes in organisations: learning and knowledge creation.* New York: Routledge.

Starkey, L. (2010). *Digital saviours: digitally able secondary school teachers in their first year of teaching.* PhD, Victoria University of Wellington, Wellington.

Starkey, L. (2010a). Teachers' pedagogical reasoning and action in the digital age. *Teachers and Teaching, 16*(2), 233–244.

Starkey, L. and McCarthy, A. (2008). *Integrating web 2.0 into a geography classroom.* Paper presented at the Australian Computers in Education Conference, Canberra.

Sternberg, R. J. (2003). What is an 'expert student'? *Educational Researcher, 32*(8), 5–9. doi: 10.3102/0013189X032008005.

Sullivan, J. P. (2009). *Emergent learning: the power of complex adaptive systems in the classroom.* Paper presented at the complexity and research in teacher education conference, University of Aberdeen, Scotland.

Tapscott, D. and Williams, A. D. (2006). *Wikinomics: how mass collaboration changes everything.* New York: Portfolio.

Tunstall, P. and Gipps, C. (1996). Teacher feedback to young children in formative assessment: a typology. *British Educational Research Journal, 22*(4), 389–404.

Villegas, A. M. (1991). Culturally responsive pedagogy of the 1990s and beyond. *Trends and Issues paper No. 6.* Washington: ERIC Clearinghouse on teacher education.

Vinge, V. (1986). *Marooned in realtime.* New York: Tor Books.

Vygotsky, L. S. (1987). *The History of the Development of Higher Mental Functions* (M. J. Hall, Trans. Vol. 4). New York: Plenum Press.

Waldrop, M. M. (1992). *Complexity: the emerging science at the edge of order and chaos.* New York: Simon and Schuster.

Weber, L. (1971). *The English infant school and informal education*. New Jersey: Prentice-Hall.

Wiggins, G. (1993). Assessment: authenticity, context and validity. *Phi Delta Kappan*, *75*(3), 200–214.

Wilson, L. and Starkey, L. (2009). Scaffolding conversational skills: why students worry about talking spontaneously and what to do about this. *The New Zealand Language Teacher*, *35*, 8–12.

Wink, J. (2000). *Critical pedagogy: notes from the real world*. Boston: Allyn & Bacon.

Index

Page numbers in *italics* denotes a figure/table

academic knowledge: and teachers 94, 95, 110–11
accountability 120, *121*; evidence based 120, 122; external 120; internal 120
Amazon 16, 106
analysis 103–4
Anderson, C. 16, 105
Argyll Commission 11, 12
Aristotle 55
artistic messages learning 86–7, *87*, *88*
assessment, student: and critical thinking 63–6; in the digital age 122–4, *123*; formative 35, 45, 92, 108, 122
assessment rubrics 44, *44*, 45, 60, 61, *61*, 71, 123
atoms and molecules learning 78–81, *81*, *89*
attribution theory 100
Australia 15
authentic learning 43, 46

back to the future learning experience model 87–90, *90*, 110, 112
badverts 60, *61*, 63
Baker, Eva 108
behaviour management plan 35–6, *36*
behaviourist learning theory 22, *23*, 28, 33
Benware, C.A. 105
Bereiter, Carl 24, 45, 46, 60–2
biological sciences, curriculum thinking within 59
Black, Paul 63, 124
Bloom, B.S. 22
Bloom's taxonomy 42, *43*, 44, 50
books, mass publication of 10–11
Borko, H. 68
Brown, M. 17, 18
Bryson, Bill 13
Butler, Ruth 64

cartoons 47
cell phones 14
Center for Research on Evaluation, Standards and Student Testing (CRESST) (US) 108
child centred teaching 43, 45, 46
cities: and urban spatial patterns learning 83–6, *85*, *86*
Clarke, S. 104
collaborative learning 32, 33, 34, 39
community: connections with local 37, *37*; importance of schools within the 117–18
completion goals 60–1
complexity theory 1–9, 12, 24, 29, 39, 47; balancing randomness and deterministic order 6–8, *7*; and change in schools 8–9; and context 3–4; and critical thinking 57; and curriculum development 12–13, *14*; diversity and redundancy 5–6, *6*, 27; and education 12, *13*; and emergent knowledge 4–5, 47; and process of change in digital age 124–6, *125*, 127; and schools 1–9, 19
computerised adaptive learning 98, 119
computerised adaptive testing 74, 122, 124
computers 8, 17, 18
concept maps 71
concepts 41–2, *42*; and curriculum 108–10; mastery of 50, *50*, 51; progression of learning 108, *109*
conceptual artefacts 45–7, *50*
Connect.ed 37
connections 29–40, 111; beyond the classroom 36–8, 40; emergence of knowledge through 4–5; with peers 32–4, *33*; teacher-student 29–32, *31*, 34, 39; to local community 37, *37*; within learning 38–9; within the learning context 34–6

connectivist learning theory 24–5, *25*, 29,
    32, 47, 49
constructivist learning theory 22–4, *23*,
    38–9, 43, 44, 45, 47, 56, 60, 92
content knowledge 94–5; pedagogical 95–6
context: and complexity theory 3–4
contextual knowledge 98
contextual learning 43
conversation skills, learning 77–8, *78*, *79*
cooperative learning 33
Cornelius-White, J. 30
Cox, M. 18
creativity: and knowledge creation
    48–9, 51
CRESST (Center for Research on
    Evaluation, Standards and Student
    Testing) 108
critical thinking 55–67, 115; about
    information, data and resources 57;
    about learning progress 59–63; and
    assessment 63–6; and complexity theory
    57; and constructivist learning 56;
    definition 55, 56; and Delphi Report 56;
    dispositions of 56; and knowledge
    creation 63, 65, 67; and learning
    concepts/skills 58–9; and positivist
    learning 55–6
Cuban, L. 18
curriculum 26–8, 95–6, 101; complexity
    theory and development of 12–13, *14*;
    and concepts and skills to be mastered
    108–10; digital age 107–10, 127; in
    industrial age 12–13, 107; and knowledge
    26–8; and knowledge creation 108–9;
    outcomes based 22, 29, 43, 47, 58, 60,
    92, 107–8; priorities within 107

data: aggregation of 113; analysis of
    103–4; and critical thinking 57; national
    progress 120–2
data projectors 17
De Bono, Edward 59
Deci, E.L. 105
Delphi Report 56
descriptive feedback 104
deterministic order, balancing 6–8, *7*
Dewey, John 5, 10, 11, 20, 42–3, 46, 127
digital age 14–19; assessment in 122–4, *123*;
    complexity theory and process of change
    in 124–6, *125*, 127; and curriculum
    107–10, 127; global significance 16–19;
    implications for educational policies
    120–4; implications for schools 117–20;
    implications for students 114–17, 127;
    implications for teachers 110–14,
    127; teaching in the 92–106

digital age learning 50–1, *51*, 68–91; artistic
    messages learning 86–7, *87*, *88*; atoms and
    molecules learning 78–81, *81*, *89*; back
    to the future learning experience model
    87–90, *90*; framework for learning 70–1,
    70; and language learning 37, 76–8, *78*, *79*;
    and motivation 68–71; places where
    learning can occur 70–1; poetry learning
    73–5, *73*, *76*; and sports coaching
    learning 81–3, *83*; storytelling 71–3, *72*,
    73; urban spatial patterns learning
    83–6, *85*, *86*
digital learning records 120
digital natives 117
digital technologies: accessing of
    information 18; categories of use 17–18;
    presentation of information 17; and
    student achievement 18; subject specific
    interactive uses 17
direct instruction 22, 35
discovery learning 43, 105
diversity 5–6, *6*, 27; in learning 101–2, *102*

ebay 16
ebooks 39
edge of chaos 5–6, 125–6
educational psychology, knowledge of 96–7
Eisenberg, M.B. 56
electronic learning records 113, 120
elite performance 81–3, *83*
emotional memory tags 97
English: curriculum thinking within 59
Ennis, R.H. 55, 56, 57
enrolment, high school (1867) *11*
environmental issue: problem
    solving 58
e-portfolios 45, 71
Ericsson, K.A. 102
essay writing 27
evaluative feedback 104
evidence based accountability model
    120, 122
evidence based teaching practice 99, *99*,
    102–3, 104–5, 112
examination process 122–3
expectancy-value theory 68, *69*, 96,
    96, 100
external accountability 122

Facione, Peter 56
feedback: descriptive 104; evaluative 104;
    features of quality 104–5; on students
    63–6, 104–5
formative assessment 35, 45, 92, 108, 122
future: back to the future learning experience
    model 87–90, *90*

gaming, online 15–16
Gawith, Gwen 56
geography students: urban spatial patterns
    learning 84–6, *85*, *86*
Gilbert, Jane 24
Gipps, Caroline 104
globalisation: impact of on food project 49
goal orientations, student 60–2
graphic organisers 71

Hattie, John 20–1, 29, 32
Hawking, Stephen 1
historical thinking 58
history studies 59–60
home economics learning 52–3, *52*

industrial age 10–13, 19, 20, 21
infant school movement 46
information: and critical thinking 57;
    digital technologies and accessing
    of 18; use of digital technologies to
    present 17
inquiry type learning *see* discovery learning
interactive learning 42–3
Internet 15, 16, 24, 98; and critical
    thinking 57; impact of on sales and
    marketing of products 105–6; and
    knowledge creation 47–8
intrinsic motivation 68, 105

Japan 12
Johnson, David and Roger 33
joke 46–7

Kirkpatrick, D. 95
knowledge: behaviourist view of 22;
    comparison of in digital and industrial
    ages *27*; and complexity theory 47;
    conditions of emergent 125–6, *126*;
    connectivist perspective 4–5, 24–5, *25*, 28,
    48, 49; constructivist view 22–4, *23*, 28;
    content 94–5; contextual 98; creation of
    within educational research 25; and
    curriculum 26–8; development of 21; of
    educational psychology 96–7; of learners
    97; and learning theories 22–6;
    pedagogical content 95–6, 105;
    perspectives of 20–2; positivist
    perspective of 21–2, 28, 35, 47, 55;
    relationship between schooling system
    and 21, *21*
knowledge building 42–3, *43*, 61–2
knowledge creation 41–54, 92, 108; and
    concepts 41–2, *42*; and conceptual artefacts
    45–7, 50, *50*; and creativity 48–9, 51; and
    critical thinking 63, 65, 67; and curriculum

108–9; home economics learning example
    52–3, *52*; and Internet 47–8; linking of
    different subject domains 53; and project
    based learning 43–4; and social networking
    sites 48; taxonomies to build conceptual
    knowledge 42–3, *43*
knowledge products 43–5, *50*

language learning 37, 76–8, *78*, *79*
laptops 17
learning: definition 68; digital age *see*
    digital age learning; diversity in 101–2,
    102; framework for 70–1, *70*; knowledge
    and theories of 22–6; prioritising teaching
    over 92–3
learning context: connections within the
    34–6
learning goals 61
learning plans 63
learning progress: critical thinking about
    59–63; evaluation of 113
Lenhart, A. 15
lifelong learning 45
Ling, R. 14
local community *see* community
long tail 16, 49, 106
long-term memory 60

Maori students: and Te Kotahitanga
    initiative 30
market day type learning activity 46, 51
Marzano, R.J. 29
mashups 39, 48, 117
mastery of concepts/skills 50, *50*, 51
mastery learning 32, 61, 99–101, *100*
memory 97; long term 60
messages: artistic messages learning
    86–7, *87*, *88*
metacognitive skills 72, 77, 115
metacognitive strategies 55, 59–60, 66,
    71, 73, 76–7, 96, 115
MIT 48
mobile devices: and language learning 78
mobile phone technologies 14–15
Morrison, K. 5
motion capture software 82
motivation 45, 68–71, 72; and
    expectancy-value theory 68–9, *69*,
    96, *96*; extrinsic 68; intrinsic 68, 105

National Advisory Committee on Creative
    and Cultural Education 48–9
national governance activity 44–5,
    50, 51–2
networks 2, 24, 29, 48, 127; learning 47,
    112; online 26; social and professional 15,

16, 41, 49, 113; teacher 91, 98, 105, 112, 114; *see also* social networking
New Zealand 12, 37, 119; Te Kotahitanga initiative 30
Ng, Evelyn 60–2
Norway 14
Nuthall, G.A. 33

online gaming 15–16
online learning 37–8, 78–9
Oppenheimer, T. 18
outcomes based curriculum 22, 29, 42, 47, 58, 60, 92, 107–8

Papert, Seymour 44
parents: relationship with teachers 117
pedagogical content knowledge 95–6, 105; technological 25–6
pedagogical reasoning 93–4, *94*
peer feedback 63, 64, 72
peer relationships: positive influence of on learning 78; and students 32–4, *33*, 39
peer tutoring: and language learning 76–7
physical education: curriculum thinking within 58; and digital age learning 81–3, *83*
Piaget, J. 43
place based learning 37, *37*
Plato 48
poetry learning 73–5, *73*, *76*, 96
policies, educational: implications of digital age for 120–4
portfolio 45, 124; e- 45, 71
positivist perspective 21–2, *23*, 24, 28, 55–6
poststructuralism 56
problem-based learning 46
project based learning 43, *43*–5, 46, 56
Putnam, R.T. 68

randomness, balancing 6–8, *7*
redundancy 5–6, *6*, 27
Roschelle, J.M. 69
rubrics, assessment 44, *44*, 45, 60, 61, *61*, 71, 123

scaffolding 24, 60, 62–3, 92
Scardamalia, M. 24
schools/schooling: aim of 11; complexity of 1–9, 19; context of 3–4; emergence of universal 13, 19; implications of digital age 117–20; important function of within the community 117–18; organisational levels within 1–2, *3*; pressure for deterministic order 7–8; purpose of 19, 20; relationship between knowledge and 21, *21*; universal access to 11

schooling hours 114
Scotland 12; education in 1864–1867 11; national curriculum 108–9
Scottish Education Act (1872) 12
Scratch 48
second language learning 76–8, *78*
self-regulated learning 62–3, *62*
Sheehan, Mark 12
Shulman, Lee 93–4, 95
Siemens, George 24, 26
Silicon Valley 8
simulation 84, 98, 122–3
social networking 15, 16, 24, 48, 58
SOLO taxonomy 42, *43*, 44, 46, 51, 100
sports coaching: and digital age learning 81–3, *83*
Stacey, R.D. 4
storytelling 71–3, *72*, *73*
student achievement: and digital technologies 18; effect of teachers on 29; impact of peers on 32, 34
student assessment *see* assessment, student
student learning records 74, 98, 103, 104, 108; electronic 113, 120
student portfolios 45, 71, 124
student timetables 115, *116*
students: goal orientations in school based learning 60–2; implication of digital age for 114–17, 127; knowledge of 97; and peer relationships 32–4, *33*, 39; relationship with teachers 29–32, *31*, 34, 39, 97, 111, 119
sustainability, learning about 100

Taiwan 9
Tapscott, D. and Williams, A.D.: *Wikinomics* 16
target setting 113
Te Kotahitanga 30
teacher-class connections 34–6, 39
teacher critique 64
teacher-parent communication 117
teacher scream *93*
teacher-student relationship 29–32, *31*, 34, 39, 97, 111–12, 119
teachers: and academic knowledge 94, 95, 110–11; beliefs about knowledge 24; effect of on student learning and achievement 20–1; implication of digital age for 110–14, 127
teaching in the digital age 92–106; and analysis 103–4; and content knowledge 94–5; and contextual knowledge 98; diversity in learning 101–2, *102*; and evidence based teaching 99, *99*, 102–3, 111; and knowledge of educational

psychology 96–7; knowledge of learners 97; and pedagogical content knowledge 95–6, 105; and pedagogical reasoning 93–4, *94*; prioritising of learning or teaching 92–3; and student feedback 104–5; teaching for mastery learning 99–101, *100*; virtual learning environment 105–6
technological pedagogical content knowledge 25–6
telephone, invention of 13
thinking aloud 59, 102
thinking hats, De Bono's 59
timetables/timetabling: flexible 119–20; student 115, *116*
Tunstall, Pat 104

university students: use of digital technologies 15
urban spatial patterns learning 83–6, *85*, *86*
urbanisation 10

value-expectancy theory *see* expectancy-value theory
videoconferencing 77
virtual learning environment 78–9, 98, 115, 119; teaching in the 105–6
Vygotsky, L.S. 24

Wiliam, Dylan 63, 124
Williams, A.D. 16
World Wide Web 16, 36, 47, 106

youth: operation within digital age 15
Yttri, B. 14

zone of proximal development (ZPD) 24